the making of
life.
of pi

A FILM | A JOURNEY

JEAN-CHRISTOPHE CASTELLI

Foreword by YANN MARTEL

Introduction by ANG LEE

NO. 1
TSIMTSUM
30 PERSONS

HARPER
DESIGN

An Imprint of HarperCollinsPublishers

to august and prosper,
who love adventures and long,
irrational numbers,
and to lisa, my constant

contents

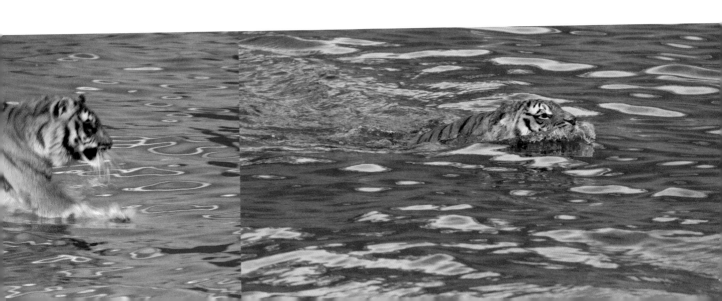

foreword

Who would have thought that this story would go so far? I had spent six months in India, backpacking and doing practical research, and then I did more academic research at McGill University's Redpath Library, in Montreal. I wasn't a student at McGill, but since I looked plausibly like one, no guard ever stopped me. I had no money. Two years before finishing my second novel I lived on ten thousand dollars a year in a ramshackle apartment with three roommates. But because I was doing exactly what I wanted to be doing, I felt like I was living the life of a prince. Imagine: my only concern every morning upon waking up was how to keep a boy and a tiger alive for one more day. When I entered my bare, little office, it was as if I were slipping into a lifeboat. Soon enough, the Pacific Ocean was sloshing around me.

My track record as a writer didn't show much promise. My first effort, a collection of short stories, sold all of eight hundred copies in Canada. My first novel did only a little better, barely breaking the threshold of a thousand copies sold. Welcome to the world of literary fiction. Still, I wrote. The artist creates out of necessity—I had to get *Life of Pi* onto the page—and so I isolated myself in my office, not only because I needed the time and the quiet to write, but also to shelter myself from the indifference of the world, a world that would have told me, "Listen, we don't need another novel, or poem, or play, or anything like that. There's plenty out there already that's very good, so stop dreaming, grow up, and get a real job."

I wrote the story in a state of near constant jubilation. It all came together so nicely. After four years, it was done. My third book, this weird story I'd concocted mixing religion and zoology, was ready to be shown to the world. What sane writer would combine the two in a novel? Most people don't like zoos; they think of them as jails for innocent animals. And most people, certainly in Quebec, where I'm from, don't like religion, at least organized religion.

Worst of all, my book came out on September 11, 2001, a day in which a tragedy of spectacular proportions made it easy to overlook the publication of a Canadian novel.

If there ever was a novel that was fated to end up quickly in the remainder pile, it was *Life of Pi*.

But we need stories. We're not just work animals, destined to eat, labor, and sleep. We're also thinking animals, and there's no better way to weave together all of our thoughts about who we are and where we're going and what it all means than through a story. In a story, we appear whole-person-like. Stories are about people in all their complexity.

The book moved slowly at first. Then it came out in the United States and Great Britain, and the pace picked up. Reviews were positive. Readers were struck. Word of mouth did its wonders. Then I won a big prize, and suddenly I was yanked out of obscurity.

I toured the United States several times, most countries of Europe, and then more far-flung places like Asia and Australia. At each stop I met readers who wanted to discuss the novel. And then there were the letters from readers from all over the world. The most common question I was asked was, "Which is the true story: the one with animals, or the one without?"

I never gave—and never give—a definitive answer. It is for each reader to decide what *Life of Pi* is about. But I'll say this: the story of Pi and Richard Parker is one of existential choice. How do you live your life? Are you directed by the flat edicts of rationality, or open to more marvelous possibilities? Do you need to know for certain, are you limited by that necessity, or are you willing to make leaps of faith?

I believe that a life without leaps of faith is a life unlived. Life is a breathless adventure that calls you to make choices, not a calculation whose risks you must hedge.

Then Hollywood came along. I was puzzled. *Life of Pi* is about a boy stranded on a lifeboat with a tiger in the middle of the Pacific. Those are easy words to write on the page. But how would one bring them to life on the screen? The challenge seemed forbidding. Who would be crazy enough to try?

To my delight, my film agent, Jerry Kalajian, believed in trying, and then producer Gil Netter and Elizabeth Gabler, president, Fox 2000 Pictures, did too. Thanks to their unwavering faith, the great Ang Lee was brought in to helm the project. Brilliant at conveying the powerful emotional detail—remember Heath Ledger hugging the shirt in *Brokeback Mountain*?—while also being able to deliver the spectacular effect—in *Crouching Tiger, Hidden Dragon*, for example—here was the director with the formidable talent needed to bring *Life of Pi* to cinematic life. I am deeply grateful to Ang for being crazy enough to take on my novel.

The poetry of cinema relies on much technical wizardry. Jean-Christophe Castelli's detailed and sumptuously illustrated book shows how both aspects of Ang Lee's movie were brought together, revealing the extraordinarily meticulous, arduous, and inspired work that turned those simple words—a boy and a tiger in a lifeboat—into cinematic magic.

The movie by Ang Lee and my novel have the same title, but each tells a slightly different story because each is told by a different author. In the end, the meaning of the story rests with you. Both the reader and the viewer must ponder the same question: Which is the better story: the one with animals, or the one without? And having decided that, what does that mean in terms of how you will live your life?

—*Yann Martel*

preface

~~~~~~~~~~~~~~~~~~~~~~~~~~~~~~

two storms

I first started working with Ang Lee in 1995. At the time, I was the story editor at Good Machine, the New York–based independent production company for all of his films, from *Pushing Hands* to *Hulk*. We were developing *The Ice Storm*, and I ended up doing period research for the film, which was set in 1975. I was of a similar age and social background as the younger kids in the movie, so the project was somewhat Proustian for me—the stale Twinkies of 1970s pop culture turned out to be my madeleines, every bite bringing back entire after-school afternoons. As pre-production drew near, I was even inspired to haul the dusty contents of my childhood bedroom up from my father's basement and donate them to the set decorators. The Earth Day '70 poster in Christina Ricci's room? That's my brief on-screen cameo.

I had come into the project thinking I was just going to be filling in Ang about the aspects of American life that would be unfamiliar to someone who hadn't grown up in the United States. A busy director would want just a few clear facts, and I worried that in my enthusiasm I had gotten a bit carried away, with binders crammed full of everything from overviews of 1970s feminism to the *TV Guide* schedule for the exact night when most of the film's action takes place. I was surprised by how intensely engaged Ang became with the research for *The Ice Storm*—the mix of big ideas (his) and lots of minutiae (mine) turned out to suit him just fine. An intense curiosity about things that lay outside his experience as well as a need to make intellectual connections between the film and its context were an integral part of his creative process.

At the same time, the research was really a kind of scaffolding behind which *The Ice Storm*'s emotional core took shape. When that process was finished, Ang put the 1970s stuff aside and went on to make an intimate, melancholy film about human desire, disappointment, loss, and at the end, perhaps, redemption. *The Ice Storm* is still full of period details, of course, from multicolored toe socks to key parties; but, for all that, it

feels surprisingly free of irony and nostalgia, thanks to Ang's combination of focused empathy and detachment, mirrored by the chilly, gamelan-inflected score from composer Mychael Danna, who came back to do the music for *Life of Pi*.

Speaking of *The Ice Storm* brings me, through fifteen-odd years of working with Ang, to *Life of Pi*. One day in 2009, Ang called and said he had just decided to do the adaptation of Yann Martel's book, and would I be interested in working on development and research? Soon after, I was immersed in Hindu lore, sea survival, and everything in between. Unlike the experience of working on *The Ice Storm*, the dominant feeling in working on *Life of Pi* came from the intense and delightful unfamiliarity of the film's world for me—this was a journey, not a trip, one which took me through a kaleidoscopic variety of topics, all the way to India on a scouting trip with Ang and writer David Magee.

But when everything started coming together, I found myself with mixed feelings (as was always my experience when working in development): thrilled that the film was really happening, but a bit frustrated to find myself once more standing on the dock waving au revoir while the ship sailed on into production without me. This time, however, I decided that I wanted to see the adventure through to the end, so I decided to write this book. Doing so would be both my ticket to Taichung, the city in Taiwan where most of the production was taking place, and also a way of getting some perspective on Ang and his work. In the process, I found myself making the peculiar transition from insider to outsider vis-à-vis the film: I had been one of the first people Ang had called to work on *Life of Pi*, and now, two years later, I found myself feeling like a bit of a stranger, wandering around the production facilities, which were located in an abandoned airport with the terminal as the main office. The whole thing was like some postapocalyptic playground out of a novel by J. G. Ballard. For the first few days, I watched

with bemusement the elaborate machinery at work—the 3-D camera that looked like a two-headed monster; the high-tech, glorified dunk tank surrounded by horizonless blue-screen walls; and the endless repetition. As I watched, I wondered what all of this could possibly have to do with the intensely personal and spiritual coming-of-age adventure that I knew as *Life of Pi*?

Everything, it turned out, as I learned over months of observing Ang and his crew at work in production and post-production. From the howling, gale-force winds that take down the *Tsimtsum* to the faintest breeze ruffling the fur of the computer-generated tiger, *Life of Pi* is, among other things, a triumph of technology. But the nature of this triumph lies in its discretion.

In the end, we are left with Pi and his story, or stories—which is Ang Lee's story. For in the course of writing this book, I suddenly felt the seemingly enormous distance between Ang's films collapsing. Seeing Suraj Sharma dancing giddily along the storm-lashed deck of the *Tsimtsum* evoked Elijah Wood jumping on the edge of the iced-over diving board and sliding down the icy pavements of suburban Connecticut in *The Ice Storm*: they are both exhilarated innocents, wide-eyed and briefly at one with something larger than themselves, even as they are poised on the edge of the abyss.

Like most prefaces, this is written last. I have already gone through the process of doing a search-and-replace in the rest of the book, substituting the more formal "Lee" for the "Ang" that I used while writing. I've allowed myself to retain my familiarity with the film's director here, and even after I leave the stage as an actor at the end of chapter one, the book cannot help but have traces of personal observation and opinion throughout. As an associate producer, *Life of Pi* was my life too, for a long while. My hope is that this fact adds an extra dimension to the book, a second story to the square foundations of the "making of" genre.

—Jean-Christophe Castelli

ABOVE: *Artist unknown. Vishnu and Lakshmi on the Great Snake. Late nineteenth century. India.*

introduction

The constant π—the ratio of a circle's circumference to its diameter—is an irrational number, one that goes on forever, never repeating and never concluding. In his novel *Life of Pi,* it seems as if Yann Martel uses π as a metaphor for the unknown, irrational nature of life. But for me, the idea of π has come to be closely related to the making of *Life of Pi.*

Rationality is like a zoo, and we humans are that unique breed of animal who have constructed our own cages—society, family, school, organized religion—and have chosen to live inside them, deliberately imposing limits as a way of protecting ourselves from the unknown, which is frightening and alluring at the same time.

Art, especially storytelling, takes a different approach to infinity than rationality. Art turns the infinite into a narrative with a beginning, middle, and end; at the same time, it allows a glimpse of the irrational and the unknown through devices such as images and metaphors. In doing so, storytelling provides reassurance, filling an emotional need that rationality denies us. But storytelling is not enough: even as we go about our rational lives, a deep part of us continues to yearn for some direct access to the unknown—we want to belong to it, to surrender to it, and to become the vessels of some power greater than ourselves.

That's where faith comes in: it is neither as limited as rationality, nor is it as messy as superstition. Faith is the way to get from the circumscribed viewpoint of the human to the irrational and the unknown. There is no bridge between the two, only a gap. To cross such a gap involves nothing less than a leap—and this leap takes place through another dimension.

LEFT: *Pi's irrational nickname, courtesy of the Life of Pi art department.*

When I first read *Life of Pi*—around 2001—I found it fascinating and mind-boggling, but I remember thinking that nobody in his right mind would make this into a movie: rationally, it would be too expensive. But on the irrational side, the book haunted me. Seven years passed, then Elizabeth Gabler, president, Fox 2000 Pictures, approached me to direct. I hesitated for a long time. Then Tom Rothman, chairman and CEO of Fox Filmed Entertainment, came in as reinforcement. He was persuasive. I was intrigued and challenged by the project. I accepted, even as I continued to have my doubts.

My first instincts were right: it was a real struggle to get *Life of Pi* made. The rational process of budgeting such a particular project was getting us nowhere. It seemed impossible, like trying to square the circle (to use another mathematical metaphor), and on more than one occasion, I was on the verge of losing faith and dropping the whole thing. Then one day (this must have been somewhere in the middle of 2009) I came to the realization that something else was needed, some other dimension, to bring *Pi* to life, to cross the huge gap between the artistic potential of the project and the actuality of getting it made.

A whole range of alternatives suggested themselves in rapid succession:

Another dimension—literally: What if we made the film in 3-D? This was long before *Avatar* had hit the theaters, and I had only the vaguest idea of what it might mean.

Another structure: What if we made storytelling part of the story itself, putting the older Pi and the writer on-screen in a framing narrative?

Another actor: What if we cast a completely unknown sixteen-year-old to play Pi—even though he would have to carry almost the entire movie on his shoulders?

Another tiger: What if we used live tigers to blend with the digitally generated Richard Parker to set the bar of realism as high as possible?

Another location: What if we shot the Indian sequences in Pondicherry and Munnar, the actual locations where *Life of Pi* takes place, even though there is absolutely no production infrastructure there?

Another wave: What if we designed and built our own wave tank, one that would go much further than any existing ones in imitating the swelling, temperamental open ocean?

And finally, another country: But which one? Where could we base the main part of the production? The United States, and many of the other countries we looked at, just didn't have the right elements.

Perhaps it was the novel itself that provided a clue, or a map, for this part of the journey. The freighter *Tsimtsum* sinks just north of the Mariana Trench, setting Pi adrift across the Pacific, toward the North American continent, along the Tropic of Cancer. The land closest to Pi's journey happens to be Taiwan, the floating island, the "zoo" where I grew up. And that's when everything finally clicked. *Life of Pi* would become a film. We would make it in Taiwan, even though no big studio production had been shot there since 1966. More than anything else, making a film there called for a tremendous leap of faith. And we took it. Call it fate, or the accident of adventure, but what had been around came around again: I returned home after a very long absence, and a circle was closed.

We had a wonderful three weeks in Pondicherry and Munnar, working with a terrific Indian crew, and two lovely days in Montreal at the end. But the bulk of the pre-production and production, more than 80 percent, took place in an abandoned airport in Taichung, Taiwan's third-largest city, along with brief side trips to the Taipei Zoo and the beaches of Kenting.

There was something truly special about this production. More than a hundred crew members from different countries came to Taiwan, many with their families, and over time adapted to Taiwanese life, even as the large local Taiwanese crew was learning the ropes of big-budget filmmaking and doing an amazing job. Language was no barrier as everyone worked together and shared meals in what used to be the airport check-in area. The set felt like a utopia of filmmakers.

I cannot overstate the part that Taiwan played in the making of *Life of Pi*: We received generous support from the General Information Office; Taichung gave us the gift of the Taichung airport and the wave tank; Pintung county— where I was born—gave us locations; the Taipei Zoo and Leofoo Village Theme Park gave us permission to film their animals. From the largest shipbuilders in the country to local industries and neighborhood vendors, people all became excited by the idea of making this impossibly big film in this small country of ours. Such an infusion of positive energy turned our production into a shared dream. The conditions that we created, with Fox's firm support, were truly special. *Life of Pi* was an adventurous and enriching

experience for all of us, as we got to work in flexible and innovative ways, not bound by business as usual, to create something unique.

Storytelling and faith are the two elements that kept this project afloat. Our journey is over. Like Pi with Richard Parker, we finally reached the other shore with our film. Now we come to the moment when we take a last look at our work and then let it leap into the world, hoping that it will generate many more stories in the hearts and minds of those who see it.

—*Ang Lee*

OPPOSITE: *Ang Lee directing Suraj Sharma in Pondicherry, India.* ABOVE: *The end of the journey: director and actor in Kenting, Taiwan, where Pi's landing was filmed.*

1 charting the course: development

Director Ang Lee and screenwriter David Magee came together over *Life of Pi* with both a shared sense of excitement about the story and skepticism that it could ever be successfully made into a film.

When Magee first picked up Yann Martel's novel, it was just for pleasure, but "by the end," he says, "I was in love with it." The screenwriter's inner adapter, which story-edits even his vacation reading, couldn't help making notes: "I didn't see how you could translate this to film. I really didn't." On the one hand, the novel grappled with huge ideas: life, death, God, the relationship between man and animal, a boy coming of age, and faith. On the other, the actual imagery was simple: after a colorful beginning in India, the reader is basically left following a tale involving only a boy, a tiger, and a boat.

How could a story so visually spare capture—and keep—a film audience's attention for a full two hours?

For Ang Lee (who, like Magee, first read the book for pleasure), *Life of Pi* was a great adventure, but at the heart of the novel, the thing that made it so compelling to so many readers, was the possibility of multiple meanings—which is not the kind of thing that big-budget blockbusters are normally made of.

But as challenging as the material was, it already had a passionate advocate in producer Gil Netter (*The Blind Side*). "I had never read anything like it," says Netter. The element of faith resonated for him, but ultimately he was moved by what he describes as "a gut thing—I was the nerdy kid who went to movies, and it's the feeling you get in a movie theatre that you can't get anywhere else. It's something I always look for." In 2002, Netter brought the book to Elizabeth Gabler, president, Fox 2000 Pictures. The studio acquired the rights, and *Life of Pi* passed through a number of incarnations before landing on Lee's desk.

When Gabler first approached Lee to do *Life of Pi* in 2008, the director was surprised by the studio's seeming willingness to respect the novel's ambiguous ending, which offers the possibility of a second story (the one without the animals that Pi tells at the end). Intrigued, Lee asked Tom Rothman, chairman and CEO of Fox Filmed Entertainment, what kind of film the studio saw *Life of Pi* as. "A family movie," was Rothman's reply. When Lee asked Rothman why he thought the story was a family movie, Rothman countered by asking Lee what happened after he read it.

"The whole family read it," Lee answered, for he had passed the novel on to his wife and two sons.

"There you go," Rothman said.

With this conversation, the two men touched upon *Life of Pi*'s unique potential as a movie: a thrilling adventure that could appeal to a wide range of viewers, a story that parents could share with their children, and a film that provoked thought and discussion.

learning to adapt: david magee's story

High up on Lee's list of writers was David Magee, whose work had impressed Gabler: "He did a fantastic adaptation [for *Finding Neverland*]. He's got a really great child's voice, but he's got a really good sense of drama."

Magee has had an unusual career path for a screenwriter. A graduate of the University of Illinois (where he studied theater around the same time as Lee did), he started out as an actor with, as he puts it, "just enough success to be constantly poor." To supplement his income, he began narrating audio books. One day, he had enough: "I said, 'this is a terrible abridgement of this book. It doesn't make sense. The characters are suddenly appearing in the scene when they weren't there before. It's awful. I mean, I could do better than this.' And the person in charge said, 'Well, do you want to try?'" Magee did, and a parallel career was born: starving actor by day, ruthless editor by night, wielding his red pencil with surgical precision to get to the essence of the material.

Five years and more than eighty audio books later, Magee emerged a different person: a writer. Magee's very first screenplay, *Finding Neverland*, about the adventures of *Peter Pan* author J. M. Barrie, was eventually made into the movie starring Johnny Depp and Kate Winslet, which earned him nominations for both an Academy Award and a Golden Globe in 2004.

me and mr. magee: two storytellers talk about storytelling

Sometime in early 2009, Magee's agent said that Lee wanted to make the film, and he wanted Magee to write the screenplay. Magee agreed because he "figured if [Lee] had some insight into it, some way, I was totally in." Lee and Magee met for a Japanese dinner to discuss their shared view of the novel's overarching theme: they both felt it was about "the different ways in which stories help us through our lives, whether they're religious stories or, quite literally, the act of storytelling itself."

For Lee, the circumstance of the story's telling, the fact that *Life of Pi* was an exchange between two people, was a fundamental part of what drove the story. "It became important to us that we really think about what it was that Pi was trying to relate to the writer," says Magee, "how he was trying to adapt his story to help this soul, you know? Because the same story might be told differently to a different person." So the writer grew into an on-screen character. The film would be framed by the writer's visit to the older Pi.

In the film, it is the writer, not the Japanese investigators depicted in the novel, who has to make a leap of faith. For Lee and Magee, whose take differs slightly from that of author Yann Martel, this leap doesn't necessarily land the listener in a religious place. Pi's *mamaji*, or "honorary uncle," sends the writer to speak with Pi in his Montreal home, implying that the story he will hear will change his world view. That's a great claim to make, one that the writer, and the audience, will have to decide for themselves. In fact, the ultimate significance of Pi's story may be not so much in the content but in the fact that it places the responsibility for its ultimate meaning in the hands of the listener. As far as David Magee is concerned, *Life of Pi* is really about the possibility of finding meaning through the structure that telling stories imposes upon the chaos of

PAGES 16–17: *Boy with tiger, adrift. To suggest the changeable ocean atmosphere, artist Alexis Rockman, who helped create the vision for the island set, poured pigments onto paper and let them bloom.*
OPPOSITE: *The first 3-D tiger? A 1903 stereoscopic print by James Ricalton of the "famous 'man-eater' at the Calcutta Zoo—devoured 200 men, women, and children before capture."*

life. It is choosing the better of Pi's two stories in the end that is life-changing—not just a matter of taste—for the writer. Having come to Pi as a creatively barren and therefore lost soul, a renewed belief in the transformative power of stories may be precisely the kind of faith he needs.

So Lee and Magee agreed: the idea of storytelling would frame the screenplay and inform the audience's interpretation of the story. As for the story itself, namely, the long stretches where the only elements on screen would be a boy and a tiger in the middle of the Pacific Ocean, Magee admits that at the time of their dinner, they had no idea how to bring that part of the book to life. Somewhat adrift, but at least in the same boat, the writer and director began slowly setting their course.

lost and found in india: looking for the voice

During the next few months, between long discussions with Lee and time spent alone in front of his computer, Magee struggled to find the right voice and tone for the screenplay. The book, after all, ranged in content from philosophical musings on religion and zoology to the slapstick silliness of a young schoolboy. How to encompass both in one screenplay? It wasn't until late June 2009, during a trip to South India that Magee, Lee, and the researcher took to gather ideas and images for shooting locations, that the screenwriter found the answer. He was sitting in the back of a van, bouncing along a

dusty road in Tamil Nadu, struggling to keep his laptop from sliding off his sweaty knees, when Lee told him that *Life of Pi* was like a children's story. Lee said, "It's got to have that wonder and adventure and fun. . . ." Hearing that, Magee thought of the novel's zoo and imagined Pi telling the story to kids about its wonders. "And I immediately got who that character was, who could tell the story. When Ang said that, I came up with that herpetologist line in the script."

> WRITER
> You were raised in a zoo?

> ADULT PI
> Born and raised—in Pondicherry, in what was the French part of India. My father Santosh Patel owned the zoo, and I was delivered on short notice by a herpetologist who was there to check on the Bengal Monitor Lizard.

EXT. PONDICHERRY ZOO, INDIA, 1961—DAY

There's a flurry of activity in the animal clinic behind the lizard. ZOO WORKERS gather in the doorway, talking excitedly. No one notices the lizard.

The zoo owner (FATHER—late 20s) hurries down the path as quickly as his heavy leg brace will allow. One of his WORKERS holds a large umbrella over father as he carries a bundle of sheets, towels, a pillow into the animal clinic. A moment later, the workers erupt in cheers and shouts of congratulations.

"MY SON! IT IS BAD TO PUT SOIL INTO THE MOUTH".

YASHODA CAUGHT KRISHNA BY THE HAND AND BROUGHT HIM INSIDE.

IT LEADS TO WORMS IN THE BELLY AND SOIL-EATING CHILDREN OFTEN FALL ILL.

HAVE YOU EATEN SOIL SUNNY! OPEN YOUR MOUTH AND SHOW IT TO ME.

NO MOTHER; I HAVEN'T EATEN SOIL AT ALL

KRISHNA RETORTED

"BUT OPEN YOUR MOUTH AND SHOW ME."

YASHODA SAID AGAIN

KRISHNA OPENED HIS MOUTH WIDE AND YASHODA WAS WONDER-STRUCK TO SEE THE ENTIRE UNIVERSE - THE SUN, THE MOON, THE STARS, THE EARTH, ETC- INSIDE KRISHNA'S MOUTH.

NOW YASHODA WAS FULLY CONVINCED THAT HER SON WAS NOT AN ORDINARY BOY BUT GOD HIMSELF

SEEING YASHODA AMAZED, KRISHNA MADE HER FORGET THIS THOUGHT THROUGH HIS DIVINE POWER.

ADULT PI (V.O.)
Mother and I were both healthy,

The lizard crawls away.

ADULT PI (V.O.)
but the poor lizard escaped and was
trampled by a frightened cassowary.
The way of karma; the way of God.

"That all came out in that moment," Magee continues, talking about how he quickly sketched the scene out right then and there, while the van wove in and out of the slower rural traffic of cows, carts, and pedestrians. "That's when I finally understood what the tone should be," Magee recalls: "charming and light, like an old-fashioned fable, while carrying a deeper, more serious message that would come out as the story progressed." This approach "would allow you to get philosophical without sounding too heavy."

This tone of lighthearted awe continues throughout the account of Pi's childhood as five-year-old Pi (Gautam Belur)

listens to the Hindu myths told by his mother, Gita Patel (played by the actress Tabassum Hasmi, known as Tabu, of *The Namesake*). Pi is captivated by his mother's bedtime story of how Yashoda, the nursemaid of baby Krishna, forced the infant's mouth open, thinking he had eaten dirt, and instead, saw "the whole complete entire universe stretching out before her."

The all-embracing spirituality of this idealized childhood Hinduism is the soil in which the seeds of curiosity about other religions (Christianity, Islam) take root and grow in Pi, who is very much his mother's child at the beginning of the film. However, the paternal asserts its presence in *Life of Pi*, as it often does in Ang Lee's films, which have grappled with father figures on and off since his beginnings as a filmmaker.

OPPOSITE LEFT: *Sketches from the film's storyboards illustrate the scene in which Pi's father hurries to the side of his wife, about to give birth to their son Pi, while an unwary monitor lizard rushes to his doom (opposite right).* ABOVE: *Nursemaid Yashoda glimpses the entire universe in baby Krishna's mouth, in artwork created for the film by Andrea Dopaso, in the style of popular Hindu comic books of the 1970s.*

In a crucial scene at the zoo, the twelve-year-old Pi (Ayush Tandon) goes into the forbidden feeding cage area and tries to make friends with a newly arrived tiger named Richard Parker by reaching out with an offering of food in his hands. Pi's father, the rationalist businessman Santosh Patel (Adil Hussain) reacts with a brutal lesson.

> PI
> Animals have souls. I've seen it in their eyes.

> FATHER
> Animals don't think like we do; people who forget that get them- selves killed. THAT TIGER IS NOT YOUR FRIEND. When you look into his eyes, you are seeing your own emotions reflected back at you, nothing more.

This is a pivotal scene: "Ang constantly referred to the moment when Pi first meets Richard Parker and finds out that this beautiful tiger is actually a meat-eating killer as

"On the surface *Life of Pi* is about philosophy, which story you believe in, what's the premise of religion. That's like the text. But somehow, the subtext came to me very clearly as being about growth. That became kind of the number one thing for me."

—ANG LEE

Pi's 'Bar Mitzvah' moment: the moment where Pi loses his innocence and suddenly sees the harsh side of the jungle," says Magee. Or as the adult Pi puts it, "things changed after the day of Appa's [father's] lesson. The world lost some of its enchantment."

What in the book was simply a lesson in the dangers of getting too close to zoo animals marks in the film a passage into full-blown adolescence: the screenplay concocts for sixteen-year-old Pi (Suraj Sharma) a fresh masala of existential questioning (reading Dostoevsky and Camus) and hormonal agitation (with a new character created for the film—his love interest, the dancer Anandi). This shift from Martel's emphasis on religion and zoology to the universal experience of growing up marks perhaps the

most significant departure from Martel's original novel. As Magee explains, "The foundations of Pi's faith begin a period of adolescent testing just before they leave India behind, so that when he embarks on the journey he has a fundamental reason to choose between alternate narratives himself. His mother's narrative of faith and his father's fact and reason-based atheism become the foundation for the two stories."

OPPOSITE TOP: *Twelve-year-old Pi (Ayush Tandon) makes an offering to Richard Parker while his brother, Ravi (Abbas Khaleeli), looks on.*
OPPOSITE BOTTOM: *Pi's mother (Tabu) comforts Pi as his father reveals Richard Parker's true nature.* ABOVE: *School's out: a heavy rain rolls off the back of an alienated teen Pi (Suraj Sharma).*

THE SPLIT-PAGE SCRIPT

Fascinated with the theme of storytelling and fearing that it might get lost among all the other plot points of the narrative, Lee decided early on to impose a peculiar format on the script: he decided to split many of the pages down the middle, with the present-time telling of the story running down the left side of the page and the adult Pi's retelling of the story running down the right. It was a formatting nightmare for Magee, but the strategy paid off. Says Magee: "You start becoming more creative in what's happening on the two different sides rather than just throwing in an insert shot and saying, 'Oh, there he is at the zoo now.'"

```
                        FATHER
           Don't go near the protests -

                         PI
                  (Headed for the door.)
            Of course not.
           _____
```

```
EXT. MONTREAL, NEAR THE          EXT. PI'S SCHOOL - DAY
PORT - CONTINUOUS
                                 End of the school day.
Pi turns from the railing and    Still raining. Pi, in
walks along the street, the      raincoat, walks out to the
Writer at his side.              street, where student
                                 bicycles are lined up by
              PI                 the hundreds.
    I had no interest in
    politics, and school was a   EXT. THE PIER/OCEAN - DAY
    bore - nothing but facts,
    fractions and French.        Long shot of a pier. Pi swims
                                 in the ocean nearby, burning
    Words and patterns that      adolescent energy.
    went on and on without
    end, just like my            EXT. UNDER THE SHIP PIER - DAY
    irrational nickname.
                                 Pi sits shirtless on one of
    I made up my own reading     the support beams beneath the
    list to keep from losing     pier, reading "L'Etranger" by
    my mind. I was always        Camus, the Pondi shoreline in
    searching for some           the background.
    greater meaning or
    purpose, never quite
    finding it....
                                 I/E. DANCE STUDIO - DAY
    And then I met Anandi.
                                 CLOSE ON ANANDI (15) radiant,
                                 graceful, eyes aglow, dancing
                                 with passionate intensity.

                                 Pi watches her, hopelessly in
                                 love, absent-mindedly drumming
                                 along. He is drumming for a
    Mother made me study music   class of a dozen female
    and one day my teacher came  students; a DANCE MASTER
    down with the flu; he asked  (female) accompanies the beat
    if I could take his place    vocally - "Tum-tikita..." etc.
    one afternoon playing
    rhythms for a dance class.   The dance master claps her
                                 hands, interrupting to teach.
                                 _____
```

Reading Camus's
The Stranger,
Pi ponders the
meaning of existence.

ideas, images, and inspirations

For Magee, the part of the story that occurs in India was "by far the hardest in the film" to write due to the sheer amount of religious and cultural references that were unfamiliar to him.

And so came the process of research: what Lee wanted at this early stage of the film's development were background facts and ideas, of course, but also, perhaps most of all, connections. The research for *Life of Pi* grew out of the book and script, and discussions with Lee and Magee; at this early stage, the process was free-associative and intuitive. Resources included books on storytelling, comparative religious studies into the nature of faith, accounts of the three major religions mentioned in the novel, Indian folktales, temple design and iconography, rituals, South Indian classical music and dance, the history of Pondicherry and French India, comic book versions of Hindu epics, Indian painting (particularly composite paintings of elephants made up of other animals, another visual motif that made its way into the film), photo essays on devotional practices and domestic ritual art such as *kolams*, and so on. Perhaps the greatest discovery of the research

period was Louis Malle's *Phantom India,* an intensely personal, seven-part documentary that the director shot over the course of four months in 1968, which provided a particularly rich mine of images and impressions.

Some of the research left a visual trace on *Life of Pi*'s surface, some of it became part of the film's subconscious, and a lot of it was simply read, duly noted, and put aside—which is how it should be, for there was a screenplay to finish and a film to make.

lee's maiden voyage: a passage to south india

In June 2009, the director, writer, and researcher flew to India for a three-week scouting trip. The itinerary included the two main *Life of Pi* locations, Pondicherry and Munnar, as well as a number of zoos, temples, schools, and other locations that were mentioned in the novel. Though Lee would go on three more trips to India before shooting the actual India portion of the film, he found many of the main locations in the course of his first visit, and the film essentially began to take a concrete shape in his mind, right down to specific shots.

the *rakhi* thread

In Mumbai, small details popped up almost immediately that would later find their places in the film's visual texture. A day after their arrival, the travelers were accosted outside the first temple that they visited by a smiling *sadhu,* a wandering holy man who, for a few rupees, tied a *rakhi,* a sacred red thread, around their wrists. Worn over a long period of time, the threads became increasingly frayed and faded—an effect that would later be replicated in the *rakhi* on Pi's wrist as an image of time passing and his ever more tenuous connection to the past.

the dancers

After Mumbai, Lee headed down to Chennai (Madras) in the southern state of Tamil Nadu to visit the Kalakshetra Foundation, an academy where the traditional Bharatanatyam style of dance and South Indian classical music are taught. Though dance is not an element in the novel, Lee had been struck by a dance-class sequence from Kalakshetra in Louis Malle's documentary *Phantom India* and wondered if there was a place for performing arts in the film.

Wading through stifling 105-degree heat, one caught glimpses of different classes being taught in small, open-air bungalows. Beginners sweated through basic steps while more advanced students moved fluidly through long pieces using facial expressions and *hastas*, or hand gestures, to evoke emotions and to tell stories. The dry stamping of bare

feet on tile and the sharp rap of the dance teacher marking out rhythm on a wooden block gave way to a swell of voices farther along: a singing teacher leading his students, his hands going up and down with the rise and fall of the vocal line. The vibrating drone of the *tanpura*, a long-necked lute, was the thread that seemed to connect the different classes on some deeper spiritual level, a reminder that the original purpose of Bharatanatyam dancing and Indian classical music was to pay homage to the gods.

Statues were scattered here and there among the buildings and trees, including a small statue of Ananta Vishnu, the great god asleep on a canopy of snakes floating on the cosmic ocean between the end of one cycle of creation and the beginning of the next. This deity would appear as the idol at the center of the temple tank ceremony sequence, the great set-piece of the film's first act.

In the end, Lee found a place for traditional dance and South Indian music in the film: the teenage Pi falls in love with a Bharatanatyam dancer, Anandi (Shravanthi Sainath). Though this love interest does not occur in the novel, Lee found it important to include it to more strongly emphasize how much Pi loses when he and his family set off to sea: not just the past of his childhood, but his future as well.

hari the hyena

Chennai was also the site of the Arignar Anna Zoological Park, the first of several zoos that were visited to look for material for the scenes set in the zoo where Pi grows up. There were hand-painted signs everywhere, displaying information about the animals and delivering warnings against teasing them.

Of all the Chennai zoo's denizens, an intelligent-looking hyena named Hari was the animal that most appealed to Lee, who watched closely as the creature loped around his enclosure, looking intensely restless and aware.

TOP: *Vishnu sleeping on a bed of snakes between cycles of creation. This is a fragment of a statue on the grounds of the Kalakshetra Foundation.* BELOW: *Hari, a spotted hyena at the Chennai zoo, bristles with curiosity at a visiting film director.*

DO NOT FEED ME, DO NOT SHOUT AT ME: INDIAN ZOO SIGNS

One of the most charming features of many Indian zoos is the profusion of signs delivering stern, even hectoring, warnings atop hand-drawn illustrations of visitors teasing animals, then being led away, injured, by grinning zookeepers. Inspired by the dozens of signs collected during various scouting trips, the film's art department created a cheerful, crude, fictional version for Santosh Patel's zoo.

At one point he suddenly stopped, the fur on his back bristling into a kind of a Mohawk, then slunk into a wading pool to cool off. For Lee, these movements—the loping, the slinking—brought to life the hyena that shares Pi's boat for a time, and that, in the movie, is named Hari, in honor of his distant cousin at the Chennai zoo.

It was also there, in the back of the tiger and hyena exhibits, that Lee first saw the zookeepers' modest quarters, hard by the feeding cages with their stark iron bars and concrete gutters. Drawn from a number of different zoos, these spaces would be reproduced by the art department for the film.

the great temple

In keeping with *Life of Pi*'s dual emphasis on zoology and religion, the group also visited a number of temples. This is where Lee was able to soak up some of the rich, heady atmosphere, at once sensual and spiritual, that made the young Pi so receptive to all things religious. Among the most spectacular of the temples visited was the Meenakshi Sundareswarar Temple in Madurai, Tamil Nadu, with its enormous *gopuram*, or gate towers, covered with countless carvings of gods, goddesses, and demons, in dozens of poses, all painted in garish Technicolor.

Every surface of the temple told a story, from the guardian gods of the outside summits to the dark hall of one thousand carved pillars, which extended in every direction, giving a visitor the sense of being in the midst of an endless narrative that had neither a beginning nor an end. The Hindu temple seemed to embrace it all, from the deepest mystery to the simplest good luck rituals. Moving toward the latter end of the spectrum, the party bought coconuts and smashed them against the slick, sticky floor of the temple: a ritual that paid homage to Ganesh, the elephant-headed Hindu god of beginnings and the remover of obstacles. For a few more rupees, David Magee received a blessing from the temple elephant, the animal's trunk touching his forehead.

the tea plants

Although the main sights had been clearly mapped out, the scouting trip also yielded a trove of small, unexpected discoveries. Lee visited the tea estates of Munnar, Kerala, because they are a major setting in the film—the backdrop for the church where young Pi discovers Christianity. The lush, green hillsides offered view after spectacular view, but as he walked along a road winding through the Madupatty Estate, the director noticed something else: the undersides of the tea plants, with their beautiful, gnarled, white trunks and roots. Fascinated, Lee asked Magee to take photo after photo, getting closer and closer until the underside of the small shrubs took on a microcosmic quality—this imagery influenced Lee's vision of the design of the mysterious, dreamlike island in the middle of the sea where Pi lands toward the end of his journey.

the great banyan

Even more important for the island sequence were the banyan trees, which Lee was already acquainted with, having grown up in tropical Taiwan. A member of the fig family, banyans start off as epiphytes, growing up around a host,

and then laterally outward, sending down roots from their branches and repeating the process over and over until a single specimen transmutes into a tangled forest. The importance of the banyan in Indian culture and mythology, not to mention the tree's strange and marvelous appearance, struck Lee, and a number of banyans were put on the itinerary.

The most spectacular tree was in Ramohalli, near Bangalore, a particularly elaborate specimen dubbed (for obvious but good reasons) "Big Banyan Tree" by the locals. More than four hundred years old and spreading across four acres, the venerable tree covers so much ground that it is impossible to tell where it originally sprouted. Though its bark is thoroughly gouged with graffiti (of the "Rajiv ♥ Priya" sort), there remains something particularly uncanny about the tree, which seems like a living metaphor for eternal life, continuously renewing itself even as everything else around it flickers and vanishes.

OPPOSITE TOP: *Screenwriter David Magee, associate producer Jean-Christophe Castelli, director Ang Lee, and scout Rakesh Mehra with the towering gates of Madurai's Meenakshi Sundareswarar Temple in the background.* ABOVE: *Tea plant, Munnar.* BELOW: *Big Banyan Tree, Ramohalli, near Bangalore, is a park unto itself.*

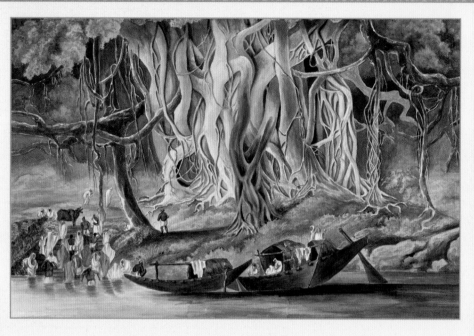

THE BANYAN TAKES ROOT

The banyan tree is one of the most sacred trees in a culture full of sacred trees and rich in mythology. In the *Mahabharata*, for example, an immortal sage named Markandeya tells how he survived the great fire and flood of universal destruction and found himself adrift, terrified, in a dark and boundless cosmic ocean. Then one day, he saw an enormous banyan tree emerging from the waters; on the spreading branch of the tree sat a radiant child—the great god Vishnu in infant form—who offered a safe haven to the weary old man. The child opened his mouth, which contained the entire universe and every creature in it that had perished from the previous cycle and would arise again in the creation to come, and Markandeya was transported inside his body.

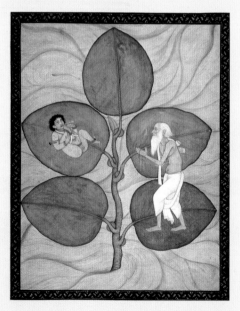

In somewhat the same fashion as the real-life tree, the image of the banyan branched out and took root across the film, from the one outside the marketplace where the adolescent Pi awkwardly approaches Anandi after the dance lesson in the beginning of the film to the mysterious island in the end, whose appearance and symbolic overtones evoke Vishnu's resting place in the cosmic ocean. (And part of the island sequence would be filmed on an actual banyan tree in Taiwan.)

ABOVE: *Artist unknown.* Landscape with Huge Banyan Tree Beside a River. *Circa 1825. India.*
LEFT: *Artist unknown.* The Vision of the Sage Markandeya. *1775–1800. Himachal Pradesh, India.*
RIGHT: *Suraj Sharma, surrounded by the banyan tree that served as a set for the island.*

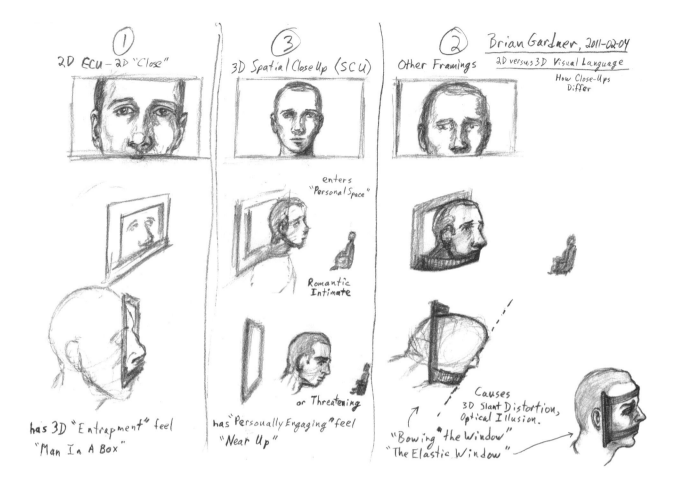

1. 2D ECU - 2D "Close"

3. 3D Spatial Close Up (SCU)

2. Other Framings

Brian Gardner, 2011-02-04
2D versus 3D Visual Language
How Close-Ups Differ

enters "Personal Space"

Romantic Intimate

or Threatening

Causes 3D Slant Distortion, Optical Illusion.

has 3D "Entrapment" feel "Man In A Box"

has "Personally Engaging" feel "Near Up"

"Bowing" the Window" "The Elastic Window"

an extra dimension: the revelation of 3-d

Another aspect of the film's development that Lee needed to contend with was the fact that it would be shot in 3-D—a first for the director. Lee had decided to shoot in 3-D long before realizing all the implications of the new technology, and the process was a continual learning curve that would carry him on a long journey all the way through production and post-production. "We're all trained to be 2-D filmmakers," says Lee. "It's very hard to get rid of 2-D thinking." And 3-D thinking proved to be an elusive goal as well.

Discussions of 3-D can get very technical, but in considering audience perception, there are two main effects that can be manipulated by the filmmakers. The first effect is depth, which depends on the distance between the left and right cameras. In live-action film, this is determined in the course of shooting: the wider the distance between the cameras, the deeper the image appears. "You can have sort of a higher setting for 3-D," cinematographer Claudio Miranda (*The Curious Case of Benjamin Button*) explains. "It can give you a little bit more of a charged sense, a bit more energy. Or you could play it subdued"—that is, reducing the separation between the cameras, which leads to a flatter image. In the years surrounding the making of *Life of Pi*, Lee noticed a general shift in 3-D films from a more conservative use of depth toward going "way big"—that is, deep shots, with plenty of in-front-of-the-screen convergence.

Convergence, the second main effect, has to do with where the eyes locate something in space. In real life, this helps to determine how close or distant something feels; in 3-D space, it has to do with where an object is perceived to be in relation to the screen. In fact, as a viewer, it's easy to forget that something kind of remarkable happens every time the lights go down and you slip on those chunky plastic glasses: suddenly, a big gaping hole in the wall of the theater opens up,

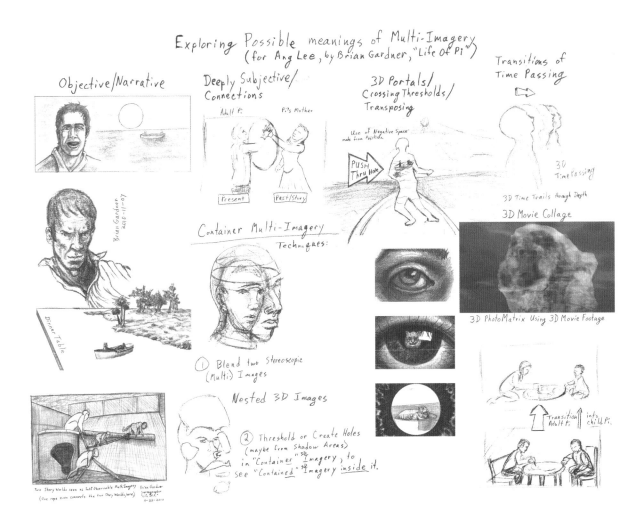

Exploring Possible meanings of Multi-Imagery
(for Ang Lee, by Brian Gardner, "Life of Pi")

Objective/Narrative

Deeply Subjective/Connections

3D Portals/Crossing Thresholds/Transposing

Transitions of Time Passing

Adult Pi   Pi's Mother

Use of Negative Space made from Positives

3D Time Passing

Present   Past/Story

PUSH Thru Hole

3D Time Trails through Depth

3D Movie Collage

Container Multi-Imagery Techniques:

3D PhotoMatrix Using 3D Movie Footage

① Blend two Stereoscopic (Multi) Images

Nested 3D Images

② Threshold or Create Holes (maybe from Shadow Areas) in "Container" Imagery, to see "Contained" Imagery inside it.

Transition Adult Pi into child Pi.

Two Story Worlds seen as Self-Observable Multi-Imagery (One rope even connects the two Story Worlds, here)

and instead of a screen, it feels as if you are facing a window. Things that are "behind" the window tend to draw the viewer out, while things in front of the window feel as if they are in the viewer's personal space. The latter is traditionally considered a more "intense" mode, though it need not be, in Lee's opinion.

Lee brought in stereographer Brian Gardner, whose track record overseeing 3-D on the animated *Coraline,* combined with his quirky, hyper-articulate views on the subject, engaged the director and helped to spur his thinking about the unfamiliar medium. Talking about 3-D in development, Lee sounds almost like an artist who is trying to grasp the physical essence of a material he has not worked with before. "I went through stages," he says, "like, is it like sculpture? Not quite." For a while, 3-D as theater was the dominant model in the director's mind: the cinematic space as a kind of proscenium, with a discrete series of planes, corresponding to stage flats in which different things could be taking place and offering multiple visual possibilities for each audience member depending on where his or her attention was focused.

Ultimately, the key lay not in adapting any one approach to 3-D but rather in tailoring it to specific moments in the film. In *Life of Pi*, Lee tried to use 3-D for expressive and dramatic purposes, rather than simply as a way of heightening the experience or making it more immersive. "I think 3-D should be manipulated, like any other aspect of film language," he says. If the dial is on eleven all the time, you lose the 3-D effect to the general tendency for the eye to become habituated—not to mention losing a powerful dramatic tool, which involves keeping the effect minimal for a while and then simply cranking it back up at the right moment, "so that when that moment hits, it will be twice as big. You will have adapted for the shallow and forgotten about the 3-D, and all of a sudden—*Bam!*—there it is," stereographer Gardner says.

OPPOSITE TOP: *Sketches comparing 2-D and 3-D close-ups by stereographer Brian Gardner.* ABOVE: *Exploring multi-imagery: theoretical sketches by Gardner.*

Two different examples of how 3-D can be modulated come in quick succession at the beginning of the *Tsimtsum* sequence. The first is the opening long shot of the *Tsimtsum* plowing through the stormy waters (entirely computer-generated), which is very deep, because when things like landscapes are seen from a distance, even in person with your own eyes, the sense of depth tends to be lost. "Just to get any depth at all in a shot like this, you have to go really wide," says Lee's longtime editor Tim Squyres. Cut to the next shot: a close-up of the face of Pi asleep fills the screen. An ominous rumble wakes him up, and "that's a very deep shot," the editor continues—almost unnaturally deep for a close-up of a face in a tight space, where the expectation would be to go relatively shallow. By going against expectations and making the shot of Pi's sleeping face feel, if anything, deeper than the previous long shot of the *Tsimtsum,* Lee establishes a link between the fate of the ship and of the boy: "It shows a bad omen," he says. "It's to kick-start the story."

The second example occurs a very short while later, when Pi, having unsuccessfully attempted to awaken his brother, leaves the room by himself to go outside. As he walks down the corridor, the convergence is on the surface of the screen and the image is relatively flat, almost 2-D. Then Pi opens the door, and "*whoosh,*" says Squyres. "Now you see the walls are way out in front of the screen." In the middle of the shot, the depth has been cranked way up, which involved physically moving the lenses apart as they were shooting the scene; and then in post-production, where it could be easily manipulated, the convergence was taken "all the way out to infinity," says Squyres. "So Pi's in front of the screen, everything's in front of the screen." The effect is vertiginous, almost physical: you can practically feel the gale-force winds blowing and, perhaps subconsciously, anticipate the breaking of the vessel. This is, or should be, a prime example of the moment being "twice as big."

But after working with the medium for a while, Lee and his editor found that even these seemingly big 3-D moments were not always predictable in their effect: "What's remarkable with something like this," says Tim Squyres, "you watch it out of context and you go, 'whoa.' And then you actually watch it in the flow of the movie—it just goes right by. You go, 'okay.' Any time somebody tells you, when you do *this* in 3-D it means *this* psychologically, be wary of that," Squyres continues. "It's all a matter of context and what the audience feels."

With its lack of horizontal motion and enclosed spaces, the post-*Tsimtsum* ocean scenes of *Life of Pi* don't readily lend themselves to traditional 3-D spectacle, which brings up the question: Why bother going to the considerable extra trouble and expense of shooting a story like *Life of Pi* in 3-D? The answer, ultimately, was found in water. Early on, Lee and Claudio Miranda, whose previous experience with 3-D was

LEFT: *During a crucial moment, Ang Lee watches Suraj Sharma's performance up close.* OPPOSITE TOP: *Calibrating the 3-D camera to insure that the left and right eye are in proper alignment—part of the lengthy setup for this sensitive equipment.*

shooting *Tron: Legacy,* conducted a test shot in 3-D of a boat with a stuffed tiger bobbing in the water off of Venice Pier in California. Miranda says, "When I showed Ang he said, 'Wow, this is the way we shoot this movie. You really feel the water's out there.'"

Miranda's pronouncement is amplified by producer David Womark: "It looks like no other water you've seen, because it has real volume to it," he says. "And that was a big revelation: you're more engaged and take the journey with the character because you're *in* the water."

"You don't have to do unrealistic, big waves to impress anybody," says Lee. "Normal-size waves can really impress you. And because they're realistic and smaller, you feel so hopelessly there, drifting up and down. With a huge, two-hundred-foot wave, you don't feel you're there. You're watching a movie."

As Lee and his crew conducted more tests they found it wasn't just water that dazzled in 3-D. "In 3-D you see more details, more nuances," Lee explains. "You see depth; the image is more worthy of staring at." A case in point was another early "3-D moment," as Womark dubs them, which happened during previsualization, or previs, a kind of computer animation widely used in the making of effects-laden films these days that allows sequences to be sketched out quickly, but with a high degree of precision and detail, incorporating lighting effects, different camera lenses, movements, angles, and so on: there was a shot of Pi looking from his raft toward the lifeboat, ordinarily a simple over-the-shoulder shot. Says Womark: "In 3-D, Ang realized that by pulling Pi a little further out of the screen"—toward the audience, that is—"it now becomes two shots in one: an over-the-shoulder and a POV. Your eyes get to choose." In other words, with 3-D,

a single shot could express, simultaneously, an objective and a subjective viewpoint. To give viewers a chance to soak in these visual details, Lee shifted his shooting style away from movement and toward longer shots.

This quality of 3-D affected, in turn, Lee's approach to performance in *Life of Pi.* "The acting should be more subtle most of the time, because you see more," he says. During production, the director would sometimes go with a regular 2-D monitor to be close to the actor for a particular scene. But then, when he watched the scene again on the 3-D monitor, he would sometimes have to go back and "reduce the performance. I think it's the proof, for me, that you pick up more details. I think more and more people will use 3-D for dramatic purposes," he adds.

finding the right currents: moving pi's journey along

Lee and Magee had found the storytelling framework for the film early on in their collaboration, and the Indian first act—Pi's childhood and adolescence—took shape through an accumulation of research, details, and impressions that gave the story visual texture and dramatic depth. This left the central and main drama to address—the long journey of the boy, the boat, and the tiger—which had to be developed in a different manner. With very few elements and no opportunity for dialogue at his disposal, Lee had to tell the story in primarily visual terms. Here, Magee's main task was to give Pi's journey a greater narrative structure for the film. "We concentrated on emphasizing three or four major developments in Pi's relation to his ordeal and to Richard Parker so that the film would carry more narrative strength without excessive voice-over."

Magee also needed to find out what it's really like to be shipwrecked: the feeling, for example, of being on a five-foot inflatable raft with nothing but a thin layer of rubber separating your bottom from the ominous bump of hungry sharks surging up from the chilly depths; of being some 450 miles from the nearest land and only days away from death by dehydration; of being alone, utterly lost in the middle of the ocean. . . .

The two sides of Callahan's experience—the knots-and-bolts of survival at sea and the accompanying spiritual transformation—became invaluable resources for the film from the very start of development. Callahan was one of the first people David Magee contacted when he and Lee were starting on the screenplay. "Ang said ideally, what he'd like is to have Steven take us out in a life raft and leave us there for a few hours. Just the two of us," says Magee with maybe just a hint of irony.

Callahan ended up arranging a somewhat more sensible day trip in a twenty-two-foot sloop off of the coast of Maine. Still, there were enough swells and "really crappy" weather to make an impression: "It inspired me to write about the horrors of being lost at sea," says Magee.

"These guys were absolutely soaked but it didn't seem to faze them, and it kind of won me over," says Callahan. For the Maine sailor, the afternoon with a famous director seemed like an enjoyable lark, a one-off encounter. "They pumped me for information," he says, and then "I thought, that was that."

Far from it. When *Life of Pi* finally left the dock many months later, Callahan would end up signing on to the project—twice, through pre-production and then production. Callahan brought not only a knowledge of the details of sailing and survival, but also a lived experience of the ocean, a deep acquaintance with its personality and shifting moods. This proved equally important in defining a broader

That wasn't the *Life of Pi*. It was the life—and nearly the death—of Steven Callahan, who wrote about the experience in his vivid memoir, *Adrift: 76 Days at Sea*. On February 4, 1982, Callahan, a naval architect, inventor, and experienced sailor, was sailing solo in a twenty-one-foot sloop of his own design—from the Canary Islands to Antigua—when it sank as a result of damage incurred during a night storm and, according to Callahan, possibly being bumped by a whale. The boat went down, along with almost all of Callahan's supplies, leaving him to spend the next two and a half months in a tiny rubber raft on the Atlantic Ocean, improvising strategies to stay alive and sane, before finally washing up on a beach in the French West Indies.

vision for the film, for as *Life of Pi* took shape, the ocean would become something like a third character in the story.

The development of the ocean as a character was partly a function of the visual nature of the film medium—if Pi could not articulate his thoughts and feelings as he does in the book, the surrounding seascape could fulfill some of that function, as an adjunct expression of his spiritual and emotional states. This was also in some ways an outgrowth of the technical requirements of a water-based film, since every step of the shoot had to be mapped out thoroughly—a way of working that went very much against Lee's usual habits at first, but became indispensable in bringing the ocean to life.

Lee has never felt comfortable with storyboards. Even on a movie as complicated as *Crouching Tiger, Hidden Dragon*, his method was "We'll see what happens on set." Lee explains that unlike, say, Alfred Hitchcock, who mapped out every shot before filming it, "I decide how to cut it, what's the best thing, on the editing table." If he used storyboards at all in the past, it was mostly as a point of reference for the art and special effects departments to begin their work.

The scenes in *Life of Pi* that were less effects-dependent were sketched out this way—if at all. Lee felt no need to previsualize much of the story that takes place in India. "That's pretty traditional filmmaking," he says, "and because I was so prepared, I already had the movie made in my head." Indeed, months after returning from his first visit to India, the director was able to describe with uncanny accuracy which view he wanted from the thousands of snapshots of tea estates that had been taken during the scouting trip in Munnar.

Even so, Lee's approach to filmmaking had already become more open to technology with his 2003 movie *Hulk*, where the technical demands forced him to, as he puts it, "previsualize it in my head." Says Lee, "I'm a dramatically trained person so I don't like that, but it was a great exercise for me. It really expanded my visual sense." Lee's experience with previs, which at that time was slow and cumbersome, had left him unimpressed, though.

But more than six years had passed since *Hulk*. The technology had become far quicker, so Lee came around. "He just started swimming and he never left," says producer David Womark, using one of many water metaphors that often seem to pop up when discussing *Life of Pi*. Working with a small team of artists from Halon, a company that had done similar work for the movie *Avatar*, Lee created a seventy-five minute animation that covered every shot of Pi's entire

ocean journey, from the sinking of the *Tsimtsum* through his departure from the island. Certain key segments were even rendered in 3-D, to test things out.

The process of previs also allowed Lee to map out the journey on a scene-by-scene basis in terms of water, waves, wind, and weather. When production time came around, the individual shots in each sequence were printed out, and the previs returned to its non-animated storyboard roots as a reference tool for each day's shooting.

To the casual observer, the previsualized *Pi* might seem a bit like an outdated video game: Pi had the frozen expression of a child's action figure, and the tiger Richard Parker moved like an angry hand puppet. But if the movie's soul was not yet formed, all the parts of the body were in place;

you could see how they worked together—and sometimes more. In the sinking of the *Tsimtsum*, the dramatic arc, the complicated choreography, and the sheer visceral impact of the storm could be felt like the rumble of thunder, still distant but unmistakable, announcing something genuinely big and powerful. With such a vision, the proverbial green light was not far beyond the horizon: after a series of increasingly detailed presentations, Fox gave the go-ahead, and in August 2010, *Life of Pi* was ready to move from development to pre-production, and from New York to Taiwan.

BELOW: *In a series of presentation artwork, Pi watches the sinking of the* Tsimtsum, *first from underwater (top), and then, a few minutes later, from a lifeboat (bottom).*

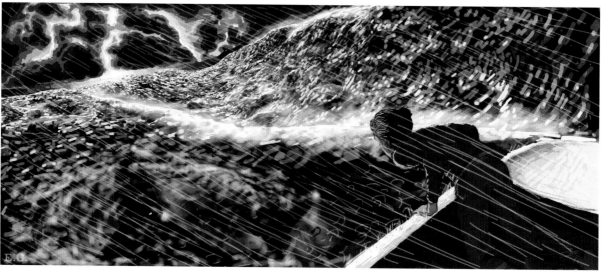

VISUALIZING THE ISLAND:
A PORTFOLIO BY ALEXIS ROCKMAN

After Lee returned from his scouting trip to India, he began to focus on how to shape and present the material in a coherent visual form. The island sequence was always the toughest part of the book to bring to life, and Lee thought it might be interesting to bring in someone from the outside to help visualize the surreal topography and details of this floating, meerkat-infested, carnivorous-plant entity.

The artist Alexis Rockman turned out to be a perfect match. Rockman, who has painted far stranger landscapes over the course of his career, brings field research, taxonomically precise brushwork, and panoramic vision to paintings that juxtapose natural history and the end of history (perhaps his most famous work is the mural *Manifest Destiny* [2003–4], first exhibited at the Brooklyn Museum, which paints a gorgeously lurid view of a post-civilization, underwater New York City).

Rockman's work was the subject of a major retrospective, *Alexis Rockman: A Fable for Tomorrow*, at the Smithsonian American Art Museum in 2010, yet the artist says that becoming a painter was actually something of a by-product of a childhood obsession with cinematic special effects. "When I started to figure out how movies like *King Kong* were made,

I realized painting was a big part of the environments the models existed in, and there's an art historical tradition they're coming out of," says Rockman. So "fine artist" became his day job, but a photo of Rockman hanging out with stop-motion animation legend Ray Harryhausen has pride of place in his studio: "Every time I went to the Amazon for real, to study real animals, I was always secretly disappointed they didn't look like Skull Island from *King Kong*," Rockman says.

With his background and obsessions, he was well suited to help Lee and art director David Gropman define the look of the island. Rockman's own iconography and recent expeditions to Tasmania and Madagascar seeped into his renditions as well: "I remember thinking about Pi's island constantly during tough rainforest hikes, and always looking at tree roots," he says.

TOP: *Studies for the island's roots.* RIGHT: *The profile of the island, with a human figure for scale. (All works are watercolor and ink on paper, except where noted.)*
PAGES 42–43, CLOCKWISE FROM TOP LEFT: *Manifest Destiny, Rockman's 8-by-24-foot mural depicting the submerged Brooklyn waterfront (oil and acrylic on panel); Pi swims in one of the island's many waterholes; a panoramic view of the island, with some interspecies cuddling that didn't make it into the film; the island's waterholes glow at night with eerie bioluminescence.*

2 setting off: pre-production

"Don't forget: It's just a boy in a boat. Easy peasy." This sign, which someone put up next to the kitchen of the production office, was probably meant as a kind of tired, late-in-the-shoot joke because although *Life of Pi* could be wryly summarized as a story about "a boy in a boat" the simplicity of the statement belies the fantastically complex technology devised to re-create the story on film—an enormous, custom-designed wave tank surrounded by state-of-the-art equipment—not to mention a crew of hundreds.

But taken literally, the statement had always been true: once the India segment of the story was complete, *Life of Pi* was "just a boy in a boat," a cast of one. A large part of the film was, and always would be, an inverted pyramid balanced on a single point, a big production resting on the slender shoulders of some young unknown actor. The big challenge at the beginning of pre-production was finding him. Because, as producer David Womark put it, with a bit of old-school Hollywood rhetoric, "without the kid, there is no film."

casting a wide net: finding pi

Casting director Avy Kaufman and her colleagues in India spent months scouring the subcontinent, from Bollywood to Indian TV to schools to the streets, looking for the perfect Pi.

For Kaufman, whose long list of credits includes *The Sixth Sense*, *The Bourne Ultimatum*, and *Brokeback Mountain*, there was one teenager who stood out from the beginning:

PLAYING PI

The following is an excerpt from the casting notes for the role of sixteen-year-old Pi.

REQUIREMENTS

The actor will need to go through some rigorous training in acting, swimming, drumming, movement, and languages. He will be required to speak Indian-accented English and French, Tamil, and short passages of Koranic Arabic and Sanskrit as well. He should be able to assume the identity of someone who is coming of age in the South India of the 1960s and 1970s, without any hint of contemporary pop culture.

a sixteen-year-old New Delhi high school student with soulful eyes and an easy grin, named Suraj Sharma. Kaufman found Sharma when a fellow casting director, who had worked with Sharma's younger brother, an aspiring actor, suggested Sharma try out for the role. Sharma, untrained as an actor, was initially reluctant: "I didn't want to really embarrass myself in front of people because I didn't know what to do," he says. But the audition, he says, "was not too hard," and he got through four rounds in the course of six months. Even as the thousands of potential candidates were being winnowed down to twenty-two, Sharma remained on Kaufman's list. "He just had something very special," she says. "He would somehow magically make each cut," says producer Womark. "Ang would go, 'I don't know, put the guy with glasses in there too.'"

The final stage was harrowing for Sharma. "I went in nervous as hell," he says about the audition in front of Lee in Mumbai, "but then Ang started talking. You know how he has this aura about him, right? Everything suddenly goes 'Shhhhhhhhh'"—Sharma moves his hand gently through the air—"you know, peaceful."

PAGES 44–45: *King as Richard Parker, framed by faux temple architecture, banyan backdrops, and an ornamental lotus pond designed in the "exotic" style of old-fashioned zoos.* OPPOSITE: *Artist unknown. Composite Man and Tiger. Late Mughal period. 1750–1800. India. The man and the tiger share essential elements, with each containing some part of the other.*

Says Womark: "From the second Suraj started reading, Ang was blown away." Sharma read Pi's monologue about the other story, the one without the animals, and Lee noticed a raw emotion welling up that was hard to fathom coming from a teenage boy who had never acted, or even wanted to act, before. When Lee and Womark showed the tape of Sharma's reading to the studio executives, it was, says Womark, "one of those weird moments when everybody just said: 'We get it.'"

But Sharma's parents, both professors, were more worried about their son's education than the fact that some Hollywood film was now riding on his participation. Kaufman spoke to Shailaja Sharma, mother to mother, about the opportunities and risks, but it was *aarati*—a traditional Indian ceremony of blessing that is performed at important transitional moments in a person's life—that ultimately sealed the deal.

guru and disciple: the *aarati* ceremony

Shortly before Sharma was to leave for Taiwan, where filming would begin, his mother asked Avy Kaufman, David Womark, and Ang Lee to gather in Lee's room at the Taj Hotel in Mumbai. There, she set up a little table with incense, a shawl, small yellow plantains, fragrant betel leaves, and other offerings. "Since Suraj was to embark on a very significant journey with Ang," Shailaja Sharma explains, "we definitely wanted to perform *aarati* for Ang and demonstrate our commitment, pride in him, respect, love, and devotion."

"Shailaja said prayers, and she lit the incense," recalls Kaufman. "Then she had this beautiful piece of material—she draped it on Ang with a prayer. Then Suraj had to kneel at Ang's feet—he touched his feet."

Explains Mrs. Sharma: "Suraj's grandmother had instructed that he should prostrate himself before Ang and accept him as his guru as he was going to be trained and educated in a new discipline by Ang." The shawl that she presented to Lee was *guru dakshina*, a kind of symbolic fee to compensate Lee for his guidance of her son. "The ceremony was in our minds very important for Suraj as it would instill in him the right attitude toward Ang and the rest of his crew, and establish the right context for the next nine months of his interactions with Ang. The experience of conducting *aarati* for Ang gave us a tremendous peace of mind and overwhelming joy."

For Lee, who comes from a culture that also reveres the master-pupil relationship, the *aarati* evoked a complex mix of emotions: "I didn't want to be this guru," he says. "But

with that ceremony, it got to me: I had to take it seriously. To somebody like me, that's a heavy burden. You don't just throw someone at someone's feet—you have to go through a lot of tests before the teacher takes you, once he takes you. Not only the tests on your talent but on your virtue, on who you are. You select each other, it's not one way." Referring to Confucian tradition, he continues, "I have to be the righteous man so Suraj can follow me, not just obey me. I have to deserve *him*." Lee smiles at the thought.

casting richard parker

The casting of Richard Parker was imbued with a kind of spirituality, too. In search of the tiger, Lee sought out trainer Thierry Le Portier, who has supplied and wrangled animals for films such as Ridley Scott's *Gladiator* and Jean-Jacques Annaud's *Two Brothers*. Lee visited Le Portier at his farmhouse

LEFT: *The Chinese character for "king." Calligraphy by Ang Lee.* OPPOSITE: *King's "head shot."* PAGES 50–51: *Tiger dive: King comes in for a watery landing.*

in southwest France, where the trainer houses his large menagerie of big cats, hyenas, and wolves. After a tour of the animal compounds, Lee sat down with Le Portier and surprised him with two questions: Did he believe in God? And why did he work as an animal trainer? And so began a long discussion that ranged from tiger training and filmmaking to life and death and the meaning of it all.

Of course, the search for Richard Parker hadn't begun with the posing of great philosophical questions, but rather, like any casting process, a simple series of head shots that Le Portier had sent to Lee. One of the tigers immediately caught the director's eye, a cat with a truly regal bearing who seemed fully to live up to his name: King. In fact, on the feline's massive forehead were bold black stripes that strongly suggested the Chinese character for "king"—"王"—a detail that delighted Lee. Le Portier, who does not speak Chinese, had named the tiger King because he had

a commanding attitude, even as a young cub. Regardless, King had Lee at "王": the director had found his feline star. "King was the most beautiful one," Le Portier says.

King was used as Richard Parker in two ways. First, as an actor in the film, he, along with three other tigers (two owned by Le Portier, one by another trainer) performed certain scene-specific actions such as jumping into the water, swatting, charging, growling, and so on. These actions were either cut into the film or used as a basis for a digitally animated version of the tiger. Secondly, King's overall physique and his markings served as the primary physical model for Richard Parker: even if the tiger on screen is entirely digital, it was modeled and animated to look exactly like King.

The decision to use both digital animation and extensive live-action footage was made very early in the planning of the film. Basing the computer-generated tiger on a real, live one—and, moreover, cutting back and forth between the

two—represented an extraordinary technical challenge, one that the production consciously set for itself. Raising the bar in this manner helped to guarantee an extra degree of realism for a story which hinges, after all, on the question of belief. The same process was applied to the digital hyena, also matched with a real, on-screen specimen provided by Le Portier.

For Lee, the process of casting King and two other Le Portier tigers, Minh and Themis, as well as a hyena, Vlad, extended to hiring their trainer, who would become an important adviser on the film—something of a guru, in fact, when it came to everything having to do with the role of Richard Parker. Hence Lee's two questions about believing in God and why Le Portier pursued animal training. To the first, Le Portier, a non-practicing Catholic, said that he did not have any answers. The second question was, in his words, "both easier and much more difficult to answer, because I can

come up with many reasons why I train animals, but I don't think I know the real reason. There's something very deep about working with animals, especially big cats," Le Portier continued, "there is also always that little something in the background while you're working, something that makes you think about life and death and—and for some, I suppose, God. I don't know. There you have it. This feeling grabbed me early on and was like a revelation." This is perhaps one of the things that Lee was searching for in his conversation with the tiger trainer—a sense of the spiritual dimension of such a relationship between human and animal.

Despite their very different backgrounds, the trainer was moved by a feeling of kinship with the director: "Ang told me that I worked with animals, with lions and tigers, for the same reason that he made films. He could give a thousand reasons why, but the explanation would never be complete."

What was supposed to be a one-day visit to check out Thierry Le Portier's menagerie extended into more than three days, during which time Lee went through the script beat by beat with the trainer. "Thierry has that same kind of strange magic that is something very basic," says David Womark. "When you talk to him, the stories come to life."

Le Portier later spent time in Taiwan during pre-production, giving further notes on the script and the previs (he did the same with the digital tiger during post-production). His suggestions, both practical and behavioral, helped to shape Richard Parker's on-screen behavior and the tiger's interaction with Pi, but overall, the trainer professed a certain admiration from the beginning for the way in which novel and script portrayed the animals he had been working with for most of his life. "I found [the novel] remarkably well-observed," he says, citing, for example, the way that Richard Parker uses the dark space underneath the tarp as a shelter and place from which he can observe and control his environment.

Having an expert like Le Portier on board helped Lee to insure accuracy. The essential difference of the tiger is at the heart of the relationship between Pi and Richard Parker in Yann Martel's novel, and preserving this tiger-human dynamic in the film adaptation was important for Lee. Through identification with Pi's story and with the help of 3-D, Lee enables the audience to feel in close proximity to one of the most revered animals in the world. This intense, physical nearness is where the two sides of the film, the spectacular and the philosophical, work hand in paw, for in the "dimensionalized" figure of the tiger Richard Parker, Pi is as close to the essential mystery of nature as he or any human being can ever get.

landing in taichung

Shortly after Lee's visit to Le Portier's compound, most of the core crew that had been assembled for *Life of Pi* moved to Taichung, Taiwan, to begin pre-production. The production offices, soundstages, and state-of-the-art water facilities were all situated on the grounds of an old, abandoned airport on the edge of the city.

Shuinan Airport was a strange place to visit during the early location scouts. The roar of air traffic had been replaced by a dead stillness, broken only by the huffing of the occasional jogger running along the weed-choked runways. The terminal building was a melancholy ruin of travel with faded posters and dusty signage, not to mention years' worth of uncollected canine refuse.

It was an unlikely facility for a big studio film—not that Taiwan was very high on the list of places to shoot in the first place. Although it had produced masterpieces of independent cinema by directors like Hou Hsiao-hsien (*A City of Sadness*), the country had not hosted a major studio picture since *The Sand Pebbles*, a Steve McQueen vehicle, in 1966.

But *Life of Pi* faced technical challenges that made a Hollywood-based production unfeasible. Other potential locations, from Spain to Australia, turned out to be no better. Eager to work with its Academy Award–winning native son, Ang Lee, Taiwan—particularly through the government's General Information Office which, by supporting his first three films, had, in Lee's words, "started my career"—stepped up to the plate in a way that would prove critical in getting the project off the ground, or in this case, into the water.

And so with all that, plus a vigorous sweep of the broom, Shuinan Airport proved to be a pretty ideal site. It was centrally located, near big-city amenities yet isolated from traffic. It offered empty hangars galore to accommodate soundstages, workshops, and a menagerie of large striped predators. There was plenty of space for production offices in the terminal building. Best of all, an endless stretch of tarmac right in back provided a perfect place for a brand new state-of-the-art wave tank: a must for a "water movie" of this size and ambition.

the big dig

In film industry talk, "water movie" is not so much a description of genre as a diagnosis of disaster: the term refers to the kind of seafaring picture that gets dragged down by bloated budgets and sinking schedules, thanks to the difficult, unpredictable nature of shooting on, in, or under water.

These pitfalls were of special concern for *Life of Pi*, where water is the primary story element: 75 percent of the script takes place on a lifeboat or raft in the middle of the ocean. The Pacific being neither pacific nor predictable, shooting Pi's journey on location was out of the question—the filmmakers needed to set up an absolutely controlled environment for the production. And so the *Life of Pi* wave tank was conceived.

Wave tanks weren't new, of course—a number of specialized ones for film shoots were already in existence. But Lee wasn't happy with any of them. One of the most common problems, notes Womark, was a kind of "bathtub effect" where waves, supposedly in mid-ocean, appeared as if they were bouncing off the sides of something—as indeed they were in more rudimentary wave tanks. Lee was also intent on avoiding the visual monotony that can occur in water movies, a risk, he knew, that Hitchcock faced in *Lifeboat* (1944). Hitchcock had worked hard to make each shot different from every other shot, story-boarding the entire film. Says Womark: "One of the things that stayed in Ang's consciousness as he started

LEFT AND OPPOSITE TOP: *An empty hangar before and after, now a multipurpose facility, with wind machine and lifeboat.* OPPOSITE BOTTOM: *During a tour, Taiwanese president Ma Ying Jeou operates the controls for the gimbal that moves Pi's lifeboat. The underwater tank is on the right, while the Montreal interior set is in the background.*

DIGGING IN: A TIME-LAPSE JOURNEY

Assistant production coordinator Josh Smith installed a camera on the roof of the Taichung air terminal that generated a time-lapse record of the building of the wave tank over the course of three and a half months. The groundbreaking ceremony took place in early October 2010, and the containers surrounding the tank were in place by the end of the year. The wave generators were installed over the first three weeks of January 2011, and the first waves were tested at the end of that time.

developing the previs was to create a strong visual sense so that constantly we're getting a change of water surfaces, lighting, and weather. He got very detailed about it."

Lee wanted an environment where he could control water and light with precision and ease. He and his crew met with Robert Schiavi, a wave-tank engineer who works with Aquatic Development Group, a company that specializes in water parks, water slides, competition swimming pools—and wave tanks. Schiavi was struck by how much Lee already knew about waves. "Ang kept referring to what he wanted as a 'swell,'" recalls Schiavi. The generation of swells, the kind of long waves that occur mid-ocean, would require a particular kind of mathematically based wave technology that went considerably beyond current wave-pool technology.

The result was an enormous pool—246 feet long by 98 feet wide by 10 feet deep—holding about 1,860,000 gallons of water. The waves were generated by a system of blowers stored inside a row of twelve boxes—"caissons," in tank talk—that had a cumulative 2,000 horsepower (the equivalent, according to Schiavi, of one monster truck, or two NASCAR engines, or thirteen average cars, or as many as 400 lawn mowers). All twelve caissons blasting away at full capacity could produce swells of more than seven feet high, and a hard rock concert noise level of 110 dBA to boot.

"It's the biggest self-generating wave tank ever built for a motion picture," says Womark, referring to the horsepower with not a little paternal pride.

The raison d'être of the wave tank was not just power but precision: the ability to generate a wide range of water textures, wave sizes, and wave shapes—a vocabulary of movement and mood. Once the tank was in place, Lee worked with technicians and consultants, constantly tinkering with the blowers, tweaking their configurations and levels of force, even as the production was well under way.

LONG SWELL SMALL					LONG SWELL MED				Ocean Swell
S	Sw 0	12s	3.5ft	A	Modest pitch-roll; small pitch-roll; beat; several small pitches; beat	Light breeze (8-10)	84B, 85B		Occasional breakers: • Wavelength = tank • Swells biggest mid-tank
S	Sw 1	13s	3.5ft	A	Pitch up; surge; beat; boat drop; 3 small pitches; beat; rise w/ small roll	Light breeze (6-8)	89-89A A90		Occasional breakers:
M	Sw 0	13s	3.5+ ft	A	Surge & gentle up pitch; pause; easy down; big & small pitch @ mid-wave peak; beat	Firm breeze (12-15)	83JMP		Occasional breakers:

ABOVE: A diagram of the tank, with patterns penciled in, and various parameters such as size, interval, height, and wind strength, and their effects on the boat. LEFT: The wave tank seen from above. The criss-crossing wires support the silks and blacks, wide sheets of fabric regulating the light for the shoot.

Boat Movement

Pitch: *the up-and-down motion of the bow and stern around the boat's center of flotation (seesaw)*

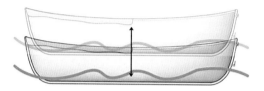

Heave: *the up-and-down motion of the entire boat, a lifting and dropping in response to a wave action (elevator)*

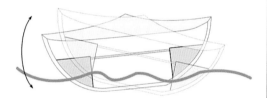

Roll: *side-to-side movement about a fore-and-aft axis (rocking)*

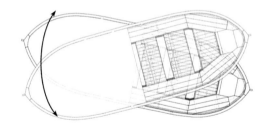

Sway: *side-to-side movement in which wave action moves the boat to either side of the course line*

Eight broad wave types emerged: rollers, split rollers, small diamonds, medium diamonds, big diamonds, long swells, left diagonals, and right diagonals.

The configurations of how the blowers were firing determined which type of wave was being generated: rollers came from all of the blowers going at the same time, producing a succession of even, rolling waves. With their relatively gentle up-and-down motion, rollers were good for representing rising winds. Going into storm mode meant summoning forth the big diamond: for this, the twelve caissons were divided into a three-six-three configuration, meaning strong alternating pressure and vacuum from the six center and six side blowers. This made the water move in a kind of "V" or diamond pattern, producing very choppy, rough waves.

Within each category, the waves could be made to vary in size, interval, and height—all of which affected Pi's boat in different and specific ways, and all of which were painstakingly noted as the tank was studied and adjusted with choreographic precision. For example, a long swell would initially cause Pi's boat to pitch up and down in a seesaw motion, then surge forward, drop back into the water, pitch up and down again slightly three times, then rise again with a small rolling motion.

As much as everyone wanted to show it off, few outsiders actually got to see the wave tank during production because it was surrounded by more than 180 cargo containers from Evergreen, a Taiwanese shipping company. Stacked five high, the containers formed a wall that could withstand both typhoon-force winds and the prying eyes of paparazzi.

ABOVE LEFT: *Ang Lee choreographs the movements of Pi's boat before a shot.* ABOVE: *Seasickness times four: a vocabulary of lifeboat motions, to facilitate the description of wave effects.*

MAKING WAVES: STORMS OF MAN AND GOD

These stills from the wave tank illustrate how different kinds of water surfaces were used in filming. The waves in each scene have both a practical, objective purpose in driving or supporting a specific on-screen action, and at the same time a subjective quality, reflecting an emotion. The big diamond waves in the example below simultaneously represent the "Storm of God"—the second cataclysmic storm in Pi's journey that throws the boy onto a new course—and his internal "storm," with his emotions reaching a breaking point.

ROLLERS

Number one rollers, medium pressure, were used here, with rounded top and gentle swell—perfect conditions for Pi to establish a rhythm alternating between side-to-side rocking and stability. The rounded bounce of the water matches Pi's punchy self-confidence as he recovers from the first great storm and begins to master his environment.

BIG DIAMOND

Number three big diamonds were used to emulate the rough, choppy seas full of pitches (seesawing), rolls (side-to-side motions), and winds building up from fifteen to thirty miles an hour. Pi's boat and raft were placed close to the caissons for maximum effect, the pressure of the blowers increasing (with assistance from wind and rain machines as well) for each stage of the storm. Impressive as they are, the storm waves in the film were used primarily as movement reference and—except for some of the chop immediately around the boat—replaced by bigger, digital versions even the *Life of Pi* wave tank couldn't generate.

MIRROR STILLNESS

In a contemplative mood, Pi floats on a reflective sea, writing a note on a page of the lifeboat's survival manual. Paradoxically, the mirror-smooth stillness that can sometimes be found in the middle of the ocean can be hard to achieve. "When there's surface waves in there, it's broken up enough that you don't see the silks [above the tank], or you don't see the blue screen," says visual effects supervisor Bill Westenhofer. "Once you get to mirror, it's a complete reflection of this incorrect world." As with its opposite extreme, huge ocean waves, mirror-smooth stillness is one of those shots in *Life of Pi* where the ocean surface is a digital creation.

Select visitors, including the president of Taiwan, Ma Ying Jeou, and the mayor of Taichung, Jason Hu, stopped by for a visit and demonstration. The containers also doubled as storage and command posts for each of the film's departments, and in the latter part of the film's production, with long periods of shooting almost exclusively in the wave tank, weeks went by when crew members barely set foot outside of their containers. The various departments tried to make themselves at home—but sound mixer Drew Kunin and his colleagues went a little further, building a full-sized patio deck in the back, which was dubbed "the Love Shack" by producer Gil Netter, who bought barbecues for the crew. To keep morale high during the long weeks filming in the Taichung tank, Netter also made trips to Costco for favorite snacks, while associate producer Michael Malone arranged for an espresso cart, and co-producer David Lee and supervising production accountant Joyce Hsieh brought local vendors of Taiwanese delicacies such as dumplings and shaved ice with fresh mango onto the set.

The fourth wall of the water tank faced west, and could be opened to admit both large equipment and the glow of a real sunset. But for the most part, the light that came in through the top of the tank was as strictly modulated as the water inside it: vast sheets of white or dark fabric—silks and blacks—were layered to mimic various shades of day and night.

TETRAPODS: PI'S OTHER FOUR-LEGGED FRIENDS

Clustered at the western end of the wave tank, opposite the caissons, were dozens of four-legged concrete objects, thrown together in a seemingly random jumble. Any marine engineer or resident of coastal Japan, where the beaches and shallow waters are littered with them, would immediately recognize these as tetrapods, designed in the 1950s to protect shorelines from incoming waves. Inside the wave tank, they served to dissipate the energy of the waves so they wouldn't bounce back and create the dreaded "bathtub effect." *Life of Pi* happened to have a fairly large surplus of the objects—which were nicknamed "Smurfs" by the crew because of their stumpy, blue demeanor—so a handful were put to work outside of the wave tank, their concrete weight used to anchor the western wall, while the rest were eventually retired to a weed-filled lot next to the water tank, looking for all the world as if they had been put out to pasture.

The top of the tank was threaded with a series of crisscrossing wires, along which moved a rig called a Spydercam, which could position the bulky 3-D camera anywhere within the rectangle of the pool, much as video cameras move above a football field to capture the action. Combined with the use of cranes, the system of wires enabled the crew to cut down on the amount of time and manpower needed to set up the shots. Below the water, marine coordinator Rick Hicks set up a web of lines (low-tech, "Fred and Barney stuff" in his gruff description), which were used to help control the boat's position and movements.

Finally, every surface on the inside of the tank was painted a vibrant chroma blue, a background that would provide the screen for an infinite variety of special effects in post-production: glowering storm clouds over huge swells, the cold scattering of stars reflected in a glassy calm, a school of flying fish surging wildly from the watery depths, and always the sea, stretching to the horizon in every direction. For all the effort that went into it, the tank was in the end a technological vanishing act, something that the audience would never see.

designing pi

A first-time traveler to India, production designer David Gropman drew upon the country's interior design style and architecture for the zoo and the Patel house, the interior of which was closely modeled on an actual house in Pondicherry, which had been in the family of filmmaker Samir Sarkar, who had helped to guide Lee around his native city.

Interestingly, it was Gropman's old-school training as a theater designer that enabled him to interact fruitfully with the 3-D side of the production. "The most significant aspect of 3-D has been what Ang said to me early on—about thinking of it as theater," Gropman says. This was an idea Lee had been discussing with stereographer Brian Gardner: how when watching a 3-D film, the viewer's eye tends to linger, to choose between details or events, rather than automatically be directed to a single point of view, as on a flat screen. Like a theatrical stage with its different flats, the 3-D space can be divided into a series of receding planes, where different events might take place simultaneously or single objects or settings may be seen. "I really tried to keep that concept in mind," says Gropman. "You know, having a proscenium, having wings, having a backdrop."

the zoo

The most theatrical of the designs for *Life of Pi* is Richard Parker's exhibit, which is almost literally a stage set, flanked by pillars with Hindu figures, with a painted backdrop that borrows from an eighteenth-century English printed landscape of India, featuring the film's iconic banyan tree in the foreground.

Behind the arcadian mural with its idealized temple (echoing Pi's statement about his childhood, that "a zoo is a paradise") lies a more sinister reality: the row of barred windows that pierce the bottom of the landscape and open into the feeding cage area in the back of the exhibit. As in every zoo, the feeding cage is where predators are separated and controlled during the bloody business of mealtime, a place of rusted bars and stained concrete gutters.

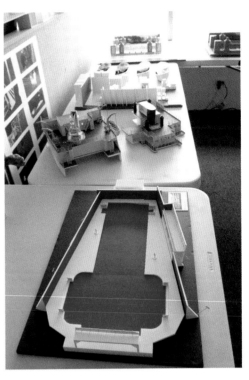

OPPOSITE: *Thomas Daniell.* Hindoo Temples at Agouree, on the River Soane. *1795. Bahar, India. The image was used as a backdrop for Richard Parker's exhibit (see pages 44–45).* ABOVE: *The model of the Richard Parker exhibit.* RIGHT: *Life of Pi on a tabletop (from front to back): Piscine Molitor, the Tsimtsum, feeding cage, lifeboats, and two versions of the Richard Parker exhibit.* BELOW: *Production designer David Gropman with Ang Lee in Pi's classroom.*

Based on a number of examples from Taiwanese and Indian zoos, the set for the feeding cage—where twelve-year-old Pi has his first moment of disillusionment—is, in Gropman's words, structured as "one portal into the next," with the 3-D effect pulling Pi, and the viewer, forward into the shadows.

Because of Indian government regulations and prohibitions against using tigers for any kind of production whatsoever, Richard Parker's exhibit—which had to accommodate King and the other tigers at various points—was built at the Taichung airport, next to the wave tank. So in the end, most of the other animals—particularly for the credit sequence—were filmed in Taiwanese zoos, with just a few simple exhibits constructed on location in the Pondicherry Botanical Gardens (where Martel places the Patel's zoo, although there has never been any such zoo there in reality). The visual centerpiece of the Pondicherry Botanical Gardens set was the front gate, which Gropman transformed into a proscenium of sorts, using a zoo entrance he had seen in Jaipur as a model and adding a series of arch-shaped flowered trellises. The art department created an assortment of suitably humorous, hand-painted warning signs, inspired by the many quirky examples that had been collected in the first scouting trip to India.

the island

David Gropman says, "I always felt what worked so brilliantly in the novel was Yann Martel's ability to make you absolutely believe everything that he told you," he says. "And so I thought, if the island wasn't based on something real, and something real that we could film, that it was going to be really, really hard."

Gropman's designs for the island followed the novel's original description of its structure, with its geometrical arrangement of ponds, while adding a look that was borrowed from the bizarrely twisted, infinitely extendable roots of banyan trees. Because of the tree's importance in the real and mythological landscape of India—the banyan serves as a visual link between Pi's lost past (he courted Anandi near a banyan tree) and the enigmatic, penultimate place of his journey (the island).

Gropman had met with artist Alexis Rockman and had seen his sketches of the island, but the designer's vision of the place finally clicked when Lee took him down to Kenting, in the south of Taiwan, on a location scout to visit an enormous, beautifully preserved banyan tree.

BELOW: *Ang Lee channeling twelve-year-old Pi at the feeding cage in a Taiwanese zoo.* OPPOSITE TOP: *The gate: the visual centerpiece of the Pondicherry Botanical Gardens set.* OPPOSITE BOTTOM: *The original gate, prior to its transformation.*

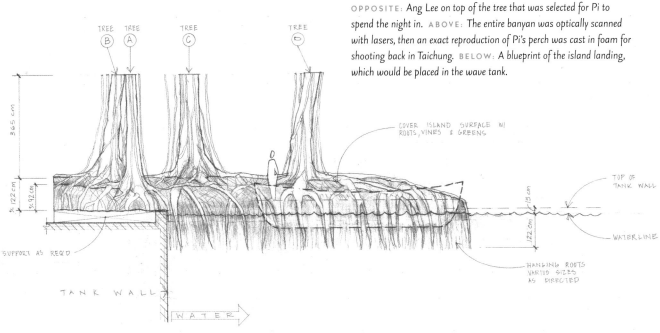

OPPOSITE: Ang Lee on top of the tree that was selected for Pi to spend the night in. ABOVE: The entire banyan was optically scanned with lasers, then an exact reproduction of Pi's perch was cast in foam for shooting back in Taichung. BELOW: A blueprint of the island landing, which would be placed in the wave tank.

TREE
B

TREE
A

TREE
C

TREE
D

365 cm

122 cm

92 cm

SUPPORT AS REQ'D

TANK WALL

WATER

COVER ISLAND SURFACE W/
ROOTS, VINES & GREENS

TOP OF
TANK WALL

15 cm

122 cm

WATERLINE

HANGING ROOTS
VARIOUS SIZES
AS DIRECTED

setting off: pre-production   65

ABOVE: The set of the island pool. LEFT: A lifeboat dangling from a cross-section of the Tsimtsum set. OPPOSITE TOP: A blueprint detail of the crank for a davit, which lowers the lifeboats into the water. OPPOSITE BOTTOM: A poster of the Tsimtsum. The action takes place on the upper decks.

"When I saw it, I thought, this is really perfect," he says. The massive tree became one of the main sets. All the art department had to do was to drape some blue screen around the edges and cover the forest floor with an extended carpeting of roots (which, ironically, were cast from some banyan trees that happened to be growing on the grounds of Taichung airport). There would be a fair amount of background manipulation in post-production—not to mention the addition of thousands of digital meerkats. Other portions of the island were constructed and shot in the studio. But, says Gropman, "Using location for part of the basis of the island gives us a real responsibility to make the sets as real and believable as the tiger."

the *tsimtsum*

For the *Tsimtsum,* the art department studied a number of vessels, using one in particular, the SS *Lane Victory* (a military cargo ship from 1945, now a museum in San Pedro, California) for a lot of the details and textures. Once filming on the *Tsimtsum*'s deck was complete, a section of the deck was put on the tarmac behind the wave tank, where it was possible to admire the meticulous craftsmanship of the set decorators, working under Anna Pinnock. Even in bright sunlight, it was nearly impossible to tell that the deck was actually painted plywood, and not the gunmetal gray steel of a World War II–era freighter corroded by years of salt spray.

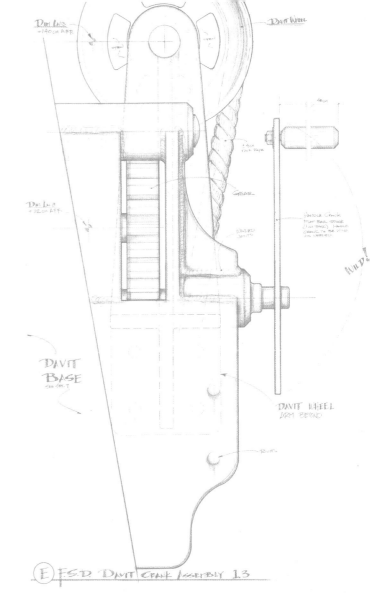

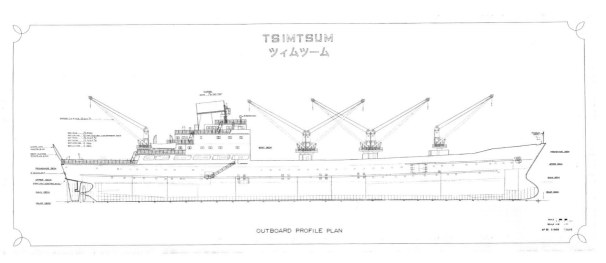

TSIMTSUM
ツィムツーム

OUTBOARD PROFILE PLAN

WAVE TANK

STEEL BOAT 1
THIS IS A TIGER BOAT

MOUNT:	WAVE TANK MOUNT (TBD)			PAINTER ROPE:	
CANVAS:	PHASE 1 2 3 4	LIFEJACKET BOXES:	2	LIFT HOOKS:	1 RUBBER
FLOORBOARDS:	HERO SIDE	GRAB RAILS:	YES	OARLOCKS:	4 HOOKS, 8 SOCKETS
SIDE TANKS:	6	CENTER TANKS:	4	STORAGE BINS:	HERO SIDE

SPECIAL NOTES:
* CAGE.
* TIGER FLOOR.
* WILD CENTER BENCH.
* BUILD SIDE BENCHES TO CAGE, 2.5' FWD OF CENTERLINE.

FIBER BOAT 1
OMIT!
(POSSIBLE STAND-BY, SHELL ONLY)
TSIMTSUM PORT DAVITS (PHASE 1) -> TRANSFORMS TO PROCESS BOAT

FIBER BOAT 3
PHASE 1

MOUNT:	WAVE TANK MOUNT (TBD)			PAINTER ROPE:	
CANVAS:	PHASE 1 2	LIFEJACKET BOXES:	2	LIFT HOOKS:	2 RUBBER
FLOORBOARDS:	FULL SET	GRAB RAILS:	YES	OARLOCKS:	4 HOOKS, 8 SOCKETS
SIDE TANKS:	6	CENTER TANKS:	4	STORAGE BINS:	2

SPECIAL NOTES:
* FULL BENCH SET.
* TRAMPOLINE, CANVAS SIDE.
* FOAM GUNWALE PAD.

FIBER BOAT 5
PHASE 2

MOUNT:	WAVE TANK MOUNT (TBD)			PAINTER ROPE:	
CANVAS:	PHASE 1 2	LIFEJACKET BOXES:	2	LIFT HOOKS:	2 RUBBER
FLOORBOARDS:	FULL SET	GRAB RAILS:	YES	OARLOCKS:	4 HOOKS, 8 SOCKETS
SIDE TANKS:	6	CENTER TANKS:	4	STORAGE BINS:	2

SPECIAL NOTES:
* FULL BENCH SET.
* TRAMPOLINE, CANVAS SIDE.
* FOAM GUNWALE PAD.

ADDT'L NOTES

* DISCUSS STUNT OAR NEEDS & FABRICATION METHOD.

* "DRESS THIS END" MEANS: DRESS 2.5' BEYOND CENTERLINE TOWARDS BOW OF BOAT.

* ALL BOATS HAVE TARP HOOKS AND LIFELINES ON HULL EXTERIOR.
  DISCUSS ADJUSTABILITY OF HARDWARE TO ALLOW TIGHTENING OF TARP.

GIMBAL
(DRY FOR WET)

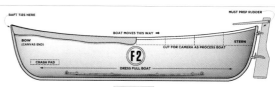

STEEL BOAT 2
THIS IS A TIGER BOAT

MOUNT:	GIMBAL			PAINTER ROPE:	
CANVAS:	PHASE 1 2 3 4	LIFEJACKET BOXES:	2	LIFT HOOKS:	1 RUBBER
FLOORBOARDS:	HERO SIDE	GRAB RAILS:	NO	OARLOCKS:	4 HOOKS, 8 SOCKETS
SIDE TANKS:	6	CENTER TANKS:	4	STORAGE BINS:	HERO SIDE

SPECIAL NOTES:
* CAGE.
* TIGER FLOOR.
* WILD CENTER BENCH.

FIBER BOAT 2
TSIMTSUM STARB'D DAVITS (PHASE 1) -> TRANSFORMS TO PHASE 1.2 PROCESS BOAT

MOUNT:	GIMBAL			PAINTER ROPE:	
CANVAS:	PHASE 1 2	LIFEJACKET BOXES:	4	LIFT HOOKS:	2 PRACTICAL!
FLOORBOARDS:	FULL SET	GRAB RAILS:	YES	OARLOCKS:	4 HOOKS, 8 SOCKETS
SIDE TANKS:	6	CENTER TANKS:	4	STORAGE BINS:	2

SPECIAL NOTES:
* THIS BOAT HANGS ON TSIMTSUM SET.
* THEN IS CONVERTED TO PROCESS BOAT.
* CUT PROCESS SECTIONS AFTER WRAP CARGO SHOOT.

PROCESS BOAT NOTES

FIBER BOAT 4
PHASE 1

MOUNT:	GIMBAL			PAINTER ROPE:	
CANVAS:	PHASE 1 2	LIFEJACKET BOXES:	4	LIFT HOOKS:	2 PRACTICAL!
FLOORBOARDS:	FULL SET	GRAB RAILS:	NO	OARLOCKS:	4 HOOKS, 8 SOCKETS
SIDE TANKS:	6	CENTER TANKS:	4	STORAGE BINS:	2

SPECIAL NOTES:
* FULL BENCH SET.
* TRAMPOLINE, CANVAS SIDE.
* FOAM GUNWALE PAD.

FIBER BOAT 6
TEST / STUNT BOAT -> PHASE 2

MOUNT:	GIMBAL			PAINTER ROPE:	
CANVAS:	PHASE 1 2 3 4	LIFEJACKET BOXES:	4	LIFT HOOKS:	2 RUBBER
FLOORBOARDS:	FULL SET	GRAB RAILS:	YES	OARLOCKS:	4 HOOKS, 8 SOCKETS
SIDE TANKS:	8	CENTER TANKS:	4	STORAGE BINS:	2

SPECIAL NOTES:
* FULL BENCH SET.
* TRAMPOLINE, CANVAS SIDE.
* FOAM GUNWALE PAD.

INSERT NOTES

* SCENE 91: PI DROPS INTO BOW UNDER TARP _____ BOAT _____ PHASE_____
  (CRASH PAD & RUBBER LIFT HOOK INSTALLED IN BOW SECTION FOR ACTOR SAFETY)

* PROCESS BOAT CUT OUT SECTIONS 1-4 FROM F2 BOAT
  SECTION 4 ASSEMBLED FOR SCENE 92, TIGER POV.

OPPOSITE: *A lifeboat tracking chart. Eight different lifeboats were used in the filming of Life of Pi, each with a specific technical function.* LEFT: *Lifeboat models. The four phases show the aging of the vessel.* BELOW: *A reference guide for Pi's calendar.*

the lifeboat

Although the *Tsimtsum* makes a mighty splash in the film, Pi's lifeboat and his raft are the most important sets. Not only are they on screen the longest, they also evolve over time—especially the raft which, like Pi, changes and grows in a way that makes it almost into a character in its own right.

The design of the lifeboat was fairly straightforward. It was based on archival drawings of steel lifeboats from the 1920s through the 1950s. Two boats were built out of steel by the biggest shipbuilders in Taiwan. A total of six more were made out of fiberglass from molds of the original steel versions. The steel lifeboats became the "tiger boats" because they could accommodate specially designed cages hidden underneath the tarp, while the fiberglass knockoffs became the "hero boats," that is, the ones manned by Suraj Sharma. Half of the "hero boats" were used in the water tank; the remainder were designated for use on gimbal—"dry for wet"

shots—that is, scenes (usually close-ups) filmed on a sound-stage, with the boat on a mechanism designed to mimic the motion of the waves. ("Dry for wet" seems kind of like a joke, however, given the number of water sprayers and dump tanks aimed at Sharma during the production.)

All the boats had to appear visually identical in every way at any given moment in the story, which brought into play another dimension of the art department's work—that of time, and the effect of its passing on the film's environment. Gropman's team assembled a portfolio of the rust, barnacles, algae, and slime that accumulate over an ocean voyage. The progressive aging of the boat's interior, under the effects of sun and salt and the gouging of the tiger's claws is, in Lee's words, "so art-directed, it's just beautiful." On the outside of the boat, the course of Pi's journey is most visibly marked in Pi's own hand, as he carves the number of his days at sea on the hull.

Pi carves the first 153 days like this.

After the raft is lost, Pi carves days 154–227 in one straight line just under the gunwale.

FINISH THIS ROW

THEN FINISH THIS ROW

THEN FINISH THIS ROW

THEN FINISH THIS ROW

THEN THIS ROW UNTIL 153 DAYS

ONE STRAIGHT LINE

LEFT: *Haan Lee floats his design in a swimming pool.*
BELOW, FROM LEFT TO RIGHT: *A raft of ideas: the prototype, and three stages of Pi's aquatic home in action.*
OPPOSITE: *A chart showing the progressive buildup of Pi's raft.*

the raft

The lifeboat design and construction for *Life of Pi* were part of a planned process, but the raft ended up being the very opposite—a kind of happy accident, a spur-of-the-moment intuition that evolved organically. Haan Lee, Ang Lee's son, was fiddling around with the design, and hit upon the idea of changing it from a square shape of four oars lashed together to a much sturdier and economical triangle of three interlocking oars. The director became very excited by this configuration, which had a simple yet iconic quality. In the words of prop master Robin Miller, "it's absolutely brilliant—I mean it's structurally solid, it's aesthetically gorgeous."

And so Haan Lee was put in charge of Pi's raft. He didn't know how to tie a proper knot, let alone survive at sea—nor did he do much research into these matters—which made him ideal for the job. Very much as Pi improvises with what he has on hand in the story, Haan Lee used available materials and stumbled onto a solution. He paddled his triangular contraption awkwardly but successfully around a Taichung swimming pool, then marine coordinator Rick Hicks took it out to sea. "It worked perfectly," says Hicks.

Working in Taichung with ropes, oars, and other material that could be scavenged from a lifeboat, Lee came up with a series of increasingly elaborate versions of the raft—each one keyed to a particular episode of Pi's journey. "As a result of figuring out the stages of the raft, I kind of became Pi, almost," Lee says. Pi's raft evolves beyond a way of staying afloat and out of the tiger's range, and into an extension of himself, a kind of narrative record of his journey improvised out of flotsam and jetsam. It is his world.

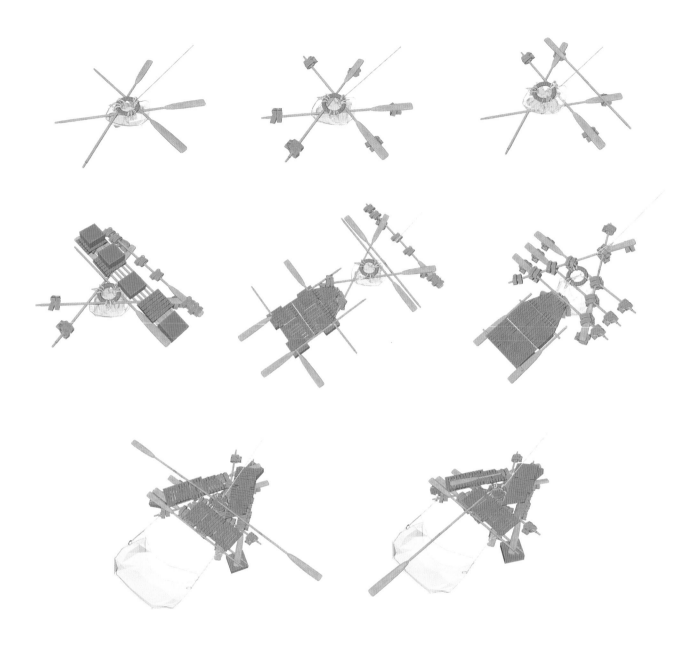

keeping it real
with steven callahan

As Pi's journey across the Pacific Ocean progresses, he conquers his initial fear, organizes his immediate environment, trains Richard Parker, and becomes, for a while at least, master of his own little world: in Ang Lee's vision, Pi re-creates the zoo in the space of the lifeboat with Richard Parker, and a domestic environment of sorts on the raft. The latter becomes festooned with all sorts of stuff the survivor has fashioned with his own hands—fishing lures made out of twisted bits of aluminum water cans and frayed nylon rope, bandannas from strips of a torn shirt, a fish spear made of a lifeboat floor slat and hyena rib bones, and so on. A sea turtle shell serves as a good shield against the whack of a tiger's paw in one scene, a pestle for grinding fish bones into powder in another, and a surprisingly elegant platter for sashimi, Pi's dietary staple once the survival biscuits run out, in yet another. The centerpiece of the raft is the combination

canopy and hammock, which protect Pi from the sun, a hard-won comfort that signifies the fragile equilibrium that Pi has achieved, completely alone, against the vast forces of nature.

These additions to the raft were designed and built by Steven Callahan, who worked with the prop department to fashion them out of materials that would have been available on the lifeboat and among the emergency supplies. Callahan came to Taichung as a consultant, but his role soon morphed into a cross between guru and jack-of-all-trades, advising the production not only about survival, but about lifeboat wear and tear, marine life, wave types (helping to develop a menu of waves for the wave tank and giving advice on what waves to use for each scene), and everything having to do with the sea.

As a seaman, survivor, and inventor, Callahan was able to expand the utility of Haan Lee's raft. "I always aim for multipurpose inventions that might logically evolve from the simplest solution," says Callahan of the canopy-cum-storage-cum-water-collection unit, which he designed during pre-production. "I made a working model (how it would furl, etc.) out of chop sticks from the mess hall and a bit of cloth from a bandage in props. We had some ideas about how this fairly

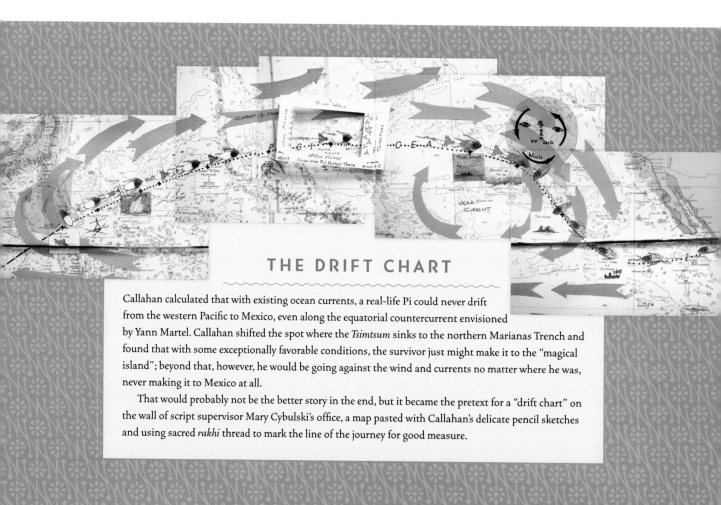

THE DRIFT CHART

Callahan calculated that with existing ocean currents, a real-life Pi could never drift from the western Pacific to Mexico, even along the equatorial countercurrent envisioned by Yann Martel. Callahan shifted the spot where the *Tsimtsum* sinks to the northern Marianas Trench and found that with some exceptionally favorable conditions, the survivor just might make it to the "magical island"; beyond that, however, he would be going against the wind and currents no matter where he was, never making it to Mexico at all.

That would probably not be the better story in the end, but it became the pretext for a "drift chart" on the wall of script supervisor Mary Cybulski's office, a map pasted with Callahan's delicate pencil sketches and using sacred *rakhi* thread to mark the line of the journey for good measure.

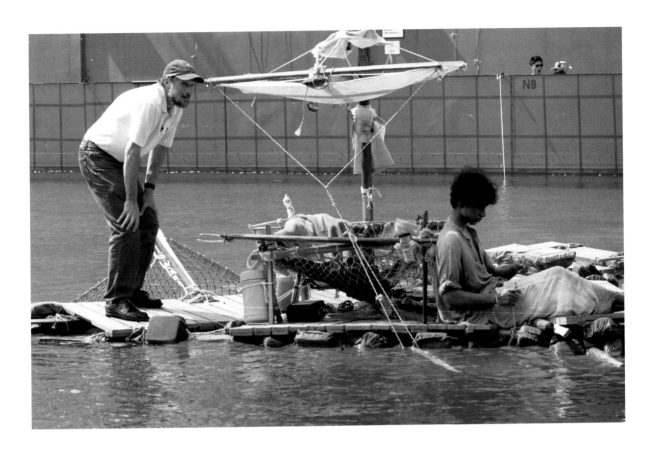

> "Part of the essence of the survivor's world is to adapt, and beyond that the making of the tools, the attention to detail is integral to the understanding of the real world. And so for me detailing of stuff is almost, can be almost like a spiritual thing in itself, that you're tied into, that this makes a difference that you wrap it this way or tie it that way, and whether you tie a decent knot or a crappy knot, that that's an expression of something. It's a very Zen-like experience."
>
> —STEVEN CALLAHAN

sophisticated device would evolve, but it wasn't until shooting that it was worked out."

"Steve kept us honest in terms of the whole survival thing," says Womark. Of course, honesty is a relative term, even when it comes to a film as thoroughly researched as *Life of Pi*. Living reality and cinematic realism are two different things—what works in life might not appear quite right on screen, a principle which Callahan sometimes found a bit frustrating: "A lot of times I'd come up and I'd go, 'Well, I would just do this, and this is the most logical solution to me,'" he says. "David Womark would come up and go, 'No,

no, that looks too neat, it looks too planned, it looks too this.' So we kind of dumbed it down a bit to make it look clumsy."

"Well, Steven started off, because he was a newbie here, just outraged at how inauthentic all this was," says prop master Robin Miller, who gently steered the seaman around the shoals of fiction filmmaking. "And we're all going, 'Steven, you'll get used to it.' I mean, you have life over here, and film over there. But he got it. You have to hold both ideas in your own mind at

ABOVE: *Steven Callahan, the man behind the canopy, watches as Suraj Sharma practices his knots.*

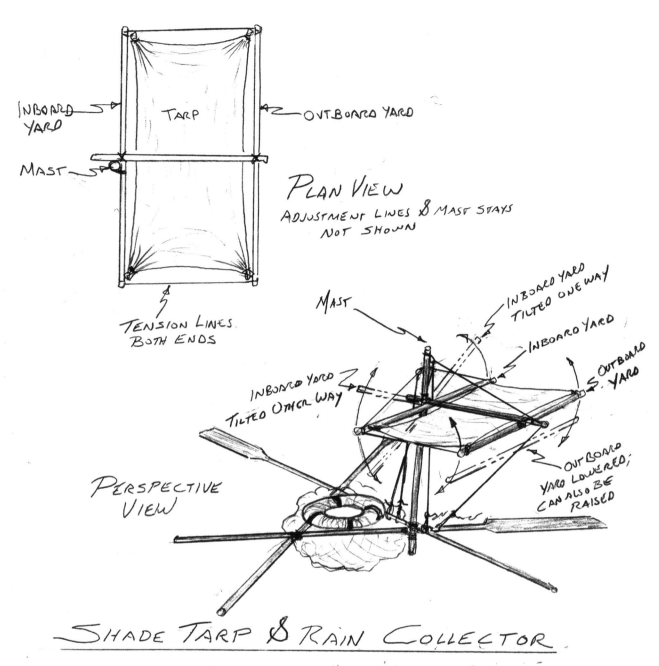

INBOARD YARD

TARP

OUTBOARD YARD

MAST

PLAN VIEW
ADJUSTMENT LINES & MAST STAYS
NOT SHOWN

TENSION LINES.
BOTH ENDS

MAST

INBOARD YARD
TILTED ONE WAY

INBOARD YARD

OUTBOARD
YARD

INBOARD YARD
TILTED OTHER WAY

OUTBOARD
YARD LOWERED;
CAN ALSO BE
RAISED

PERSPECTIVE
VIEW

SHADE TARP & RAIN COLLECTOR

- MAST STAYS NOT SHOWN
  FOR CLARITY

- ADJUSTABLE VIA LINES
  - TILTS FORWARD OR AFT
  - TILTS UP OR DOWN
  - ALSO CAN SWIVEL

TARP COULD MEASURE APPROX. 5' x 5'
  LEAVING 6"± OF POLES STICKING
  OUT ON EACH END; OR RECTANGLE
  TO SUIT AS SHOWN

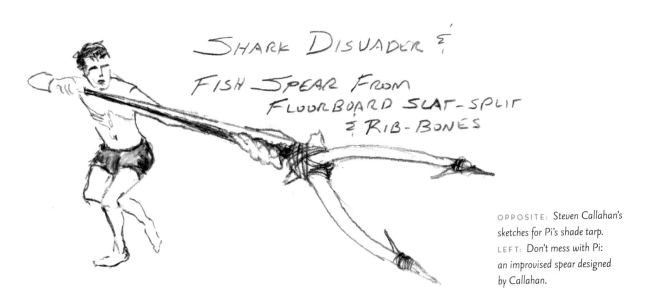

SHARK DISUADER &
FISH SPEAR FROM
FLOORBOARD SLAT-SPLIT
& RIB-BONES

the same time." Callahan eventually did, with a dose of irony: "Ang would say to me, 'Remember, Pi's not you, Pi's not you,'" he says. "So it occurred to me that what Pi is in terms of the story is that he's kind of like Spiderman at sea, really. . . . All of a sudden, he's thrown into this survival world and he doesn't know what's going on, and he may bang into a few buildings at first—but within minutes he's flying down the streets attached to these tall buildings with a thread, with no problem."

preparing pi

Suraj Sharma, whose main job description after "acting" might as well have been "getting dunked repeatedly," came to Taiwan not knowing how to swim. But that changed quickly: not only did Sharma learn how to swim in a short period of time, but he learned how to perform all of his own aquatic stunts, too. Was the bespectacled, teenage Suraj Sharma who arrived in Taichung really some kind of Peter Parker with latent Spiderman tendencies?

Well, not quite. The kid had an uncanny talent for sure, but just as important, he had stunt coordinator Charlie Croughwell and his stuntman son Cameron, who gave him a splash course in staying afloat. After a period of pool training, Croughwell and son took Sharma five hundred yards off shore. "It was important that he learn what it would be like to be out in the middle of the ocean," Croughwell says. "And he learned quickly, in one fell swoop."

In fact, the stunt coordinator and his son became a surrogate family of sorts for Sharma during the course of the shoot, even as they whipped him into shape both in and out of the water. In other films in which actors have had to undergo a physical transformation of this sort, the entire production would often go on hiatus (in the case of *Cast Away,* director Robert Zemeckis took a long break to film *What Lies Beneath* with the same crew, to give Tom Hanks time to lose the necessary weight). *Life of Pi* could not afford to do this, and so Sharma, an untested member of the most undisciplined age group, was going to lose weight in real time. The 5-foot-9½-inch Sharma arrived in Taiwan weighing 130 pounds (59 kilograms). Over the next two months, up until the start of photography in January 2010, he had to put on weight, and then lose all of it (and then some).

Suraj Sharma's days were tightly packed, for even when he was sweating and swimming, he was busy growing his inner Pi. Even without the *aarati* ceremony that officially anointed Ang Lee as Sharma's guru, the director had always taken his role as mentor and teacher very seriously. "Teaching and learning complement each other," Lee says. "I always feel that, when I teach those young actors, I'm learning about my own skill." Lee did most of the acting coaching himself, with the help of David Magee, who was in Taichung at that time. They did scenes from selected plays—*Zoo Story* by Edward Albee, Tennessee Williams's *The Glass Menagerie*—but most of the work that Lee had Sharma do involved immersing himself into his character. "We were drawing Pi in my head," says Sharma, "Ang used to make me do all these exercises, he used to make me drop my mental age from eighteen or seventeen to fourteen or twelve.

PI'S SURVIVAL MANUAL

When Steven Callahan came to Taichung, he brought along a collection of sea survival manuals. He, art director David Gropman, prop master Robin Miller, and illustrator Joanna Bush worked together to invent a survival manual for Pi. With more than fifty pages of text and charts, their *Survival at Sea: Lifeboat Manual and Navigation Guide* is more than just a prop, it is almost a veritable manual in its own right. Like all true survivors, Pi doesn't follow the guide literally, but improvises his own tools and techniques culled from it. The book's physical pages also provide a convenient surface on which Pi can write down his thoughts, to motivate the use of voice-over in the film.

   Survival at Sea might not actually get a stranded soul on a raft across the Pacific Ocean, but some of the beautifully rendered diagrams and charts, few of which are seen on screen, provide an elegant inventory of Pi's world.

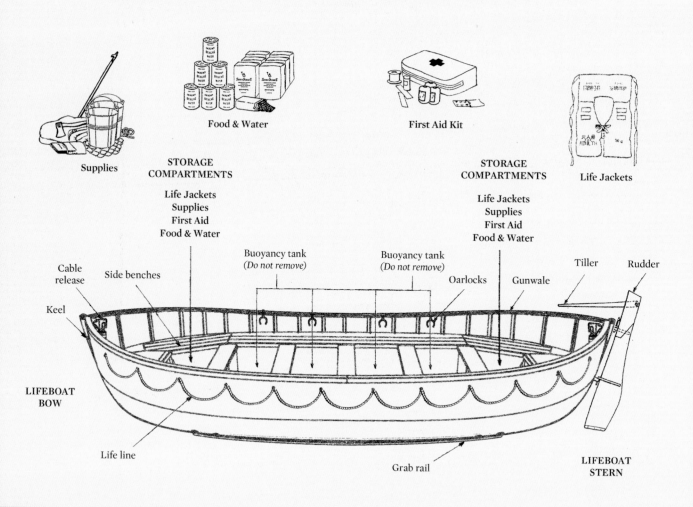

Supplies

Food & Water

First Aid Kit

Life Jackets

STORAGE COMPARTMENTS

Life Jackets
Supplies
First Aid
Food & Water

STORAGE COMPARTMENTS

Life Jackets
Supplies
First Aid
Food & Water

Cable release

Side benches

Keel

Buoyancy tank *(Do not remove)*

Buoyancy tank *(Do not remove)*

Oarlocks

Gunwale

Tiller

Rudder

LIFEBOAT BOW

Life line

Grab rail

LIFEBOAT STERN

Table III - List of equipment for standard life saving aboard a lifeboat or liferaft.

No.	Name, Standard	Quantity	Sketch	✓
1	Life ring	1		
2	Life jacket	30		
3	Cargo net	1		
4	Fishing net	1		
5	Orange smoke signals	1 set		
6	Signaling mirror	1		
7	Flare gun and cartridges	1		
8	Hand flares	2		
9	Rocket parachute flares	1		
10	Oar	9		
11	Boat hook	1		
12	Sharpening stone	1		
13	Knife	1		
14	Bucket	4		
15	Hatchet	1		
16	Compass	1		
17	Sea anchor	2		
18	Flashlight	1		
19	Rope (buoyant)	1		
20	Rope (non-buoyant)	1		
21	Waterproof matches	1 box		
22	Fishing Tackle	1 set		
23	Sewing kit	1 set		
24	Graduated drinking vessel	1		
25	Solar stills	2		
26	First-aid outfit	1		
27	Seasickness tablets	192		
28	Seasickness bags	32		
29	Storm oil	4		
30	Tin openers	3		
31	Metal file	1		
32	Yellow sponges	2		
33	Whistle	30		
34	Survival guide	1		
35	Pencil	1		

CONIC SHAPED SEA ANCHOR

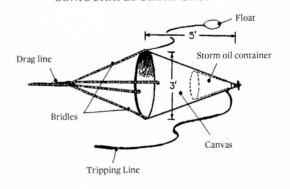

Float
Drag line
Storm oil container
Bridles
Canvas
Tripping Line
5′
3′

MARY'S PI CHART

"He's all about detail," says Mary Cybulski about Ang Lee. As script supervisor on a number of Lee's films going back to *The Ice Storm*, "detail" has been Cybulski's job, if not her middle name.

Before production began, Cybulski made a chart of Pi's journey—the chart to beat all the other charts in a working environment surrounded by inspiration walls, mood boards, calendars, and timelines. Her small, windowless office was covered floor-to-ceiling with the through-lines of Pi's journey: action, theme, Pi's physical health, his skin and hair, his clothes, his mental state, his spiritual state, his acquisition of skills, his "becoming a tiger" (Richard Parker also got his own line), the state of the lifeboat, the stage of the raft constructions, and which props were needed. Finally, the last three lines of the chart covered the waves, wind, and sky associated with each scene.

Overall, Pi's emotions are the starting point of every scene, and the chart made it clear how much the work of each department—costumes, hair and makeup, and so on followed Pi's trajectory. All the film's details are grounded in physical reality and at the same time heightened to become an expression of "how healthy he is, how close to God he is, how close he is to being Richard Parker—all those things kind of braid together," says Cybulski. "It was an idea that Ang had, because it was like he wanted to see it all," she adds. "That's his idea—to see it all."

I'd just keep walking around the room and he'd make me do that, and slowly he'd say, 'now stop.' Then he'd make me start doing things as Pi, and the way he made me do it, I started automatically developing habits and certain thinking processes which are different in Pi and me. Now it's become kind of like the switch for me, so then I don't have to act, really, I just do it."

The first time Lee had met Sharma—at the final audition which won the sixteen-year-old boy the part of Pi—he found in him a quality of extraordinary responsiveness that he had encountered very rarely in his career. "I gave him just one direction, to just describe the scene vividly, like he has seen it and experienced it, that's all," says Lee. "Suraj just took directions. To me that's the biggest talent in acting, that the actors believe in the situation given, they don't have to perform it. They totally transform themselves into what they're playing."

For Lee, the director's job also involves a responsibility toward actors, particularly the younger, less experienced ones: "Sometimes you have to watch out," he says. "A situation can really hurt an actor, and you have to bring them out of it." Even when outside trainers were brought in, Lee remained close to and often part of the process. When Elias Alouf, a former oil-rig diver from Lebanon who was now a Taichung–based yoga teacher, came to help Sharma find his spiritual inner tiger—"that focus, that clarity, that determination," in Alouf's words—Lee joined the sessions, which lasted up to four hours a day. "He sacrificed a lot of his time and energy to be part of that," says Alouf (who was cast in the brief role of Mamaji, Pi's swimming pool–obsessed uncle).

It was Lee's shared participation in the training that played such a fundamental role in preparing and transforming Sharma—and Lee as well. "I would say there's a very deep emotional connection between Ang and Suraj," says David Womark. "And a level of trust for both of them. That came from the training. Suraj did yoga. Ang did yoga. Suraj had to go in the ocean. Ang went in the ocean with him. You know Ang as a filmmaker—he goes through the journey himself."

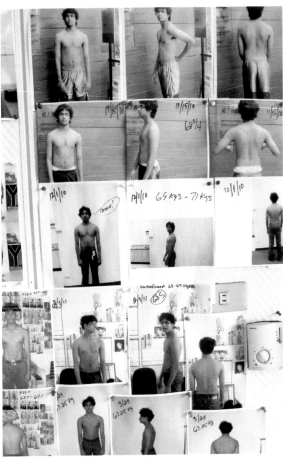

TOP: *Life of pushups: Sharma in training.* ABOVE: *The Suraj Sharma before-and-after wall in stunt coordinator Charlie Croughwell's office.*

LEFT: *Suraj Sharma paddles behind one of the raft prototypes while Ang Lee takes a break.*

3 the journey: production

On January 3, 2010, a table with various offerings, including tea, oranges, mineral water, flowers, and a centerpiece of Taiwan's exceptionally sweet pineapples, all laid out over a cloth of bright red (the color of happiness in Chinese culture), was set up facing south on the tarmac outside one of the old Taichung Airport hangars, now transformed into a soundstage. The cast and crew of *Life of Pi* gathered with sticks of incense in their hands, director Ang Lee said a prayer and, following his lead, everyone bowed to the four cardinal directions—south, east, west, and north. Then, a resounding stroke of the gong—to scare away evil spirits—sliced through the sandalwood-scented air, Lee yelled "Action," the camera rolled for a few seconds, and day one of production on *Life of Pi* officially began.

This ritual is known as the big luck ceremony, which has marked the beginning of shooting of every Ang Lee film since his very first, *Pushing Hands*. An adaptation of an old Chinese tradition, where offerings are made to the gods and spirits to help ensure a successful production, a traditional big luck ceremony calls for "whole fish, suckling pig, and chicken," says co-producer David Lee, who has participated in these rituals with Lee since *Sense and Sensibility* (1995). "But after *The Ice Storm*, Ang didn't want to kill anything, so now we use vegetables, flowers, and fruits only."

Countless sticks of incense were burned over the course of *Life of Pi*'s production, as the table of offerings was brought out for every move from one set or one location to another. As for the spiritual content of the ceremonies, Lee kept them deliberately vague and open: "I don't tell anyone who to pray to. It's a moment of quiet. You never ask for good luck," he says, "just the important small things, like safety and smoothness. It's like you don't pray to God to win the lottery, you say 'give me strength.' It's the same principle."

"For every location on this movie, every stage, every time we went anyplace, we thanked the gods. And I will tell you something: this is the first water movie in the entire history of filmmaking to come close to its schedule."

—DAVID WOMARK, PRODUCER, ON BIG LUCK CEREMONIES

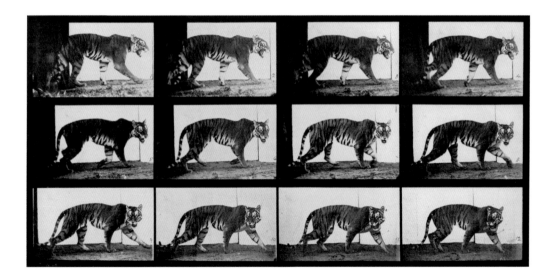

PAGES 82–83: *The float festival scene, staged at an ancient Hindu temple near Pondicherry. A statue of Vishnu, reclining on his bed of snakes, is ferried across the lantern-filled waters of the temple tank, accompanied by a group of Brahmin priests and musicians, while thousands of worshippers, among them five-year-old Pi, look on.* OPPOSITE: *Tiger in motion: Eadweard Muybridge. Animal Locomotion, Plate 729. 1887.* ABOVE: *Luck of Pi: cast and crew raise incense over a table of symbolic offerings.* RIGHT: *Ang Lee strikes the gong to drive away evil spirits, invigorate the crew, and signal the start of production.*

the *tsimtsum* sinking sequence: starting with a splash

Most film productions, when faced with an inexperienced lead actor like Suraj Sharma, might opt to shoot something short and straightforward first—a quiet domestic scene without too much dialogue, perhaps—so that the untested performer can ease into his part. But *Life of Pi* dove straight off the deep end, with the *Tsimtsum* sinking sequence instead. "*Tsimtsum* sinking sequence" makes a good tongue twister, but it's not the most auspicious way to kick off a long film shoot. This scene, where the freighter disappears into the deepest part of the Pacific Ocean, taking with it Pi's family and everything he has ever known (with the exception of a certain tiger, that is), was among the most technically demanding and physically challenging.

LEFT: *A giant gimbal, designed to mimic the motion of the storm, underneath the set of Tsimtsum's upper deck.* TOP: *At full throttle, wind machines can blow at gale force.* ABOVE: *Water cannons shoot air-pressurized water to simulate ocean spray.*

"That it was shot first up was almost mad," says first assistant director William Connor, "but we had no other choice," he explains. "If Sharma was going to lose weight over the course of the production, to match the shipwrecked Pi's weight loss, then starting the shoot at his peak weight was imperative."

So on day two of the shoot—indeed, on day two of his life as an actor—Suraj Sharma found himself standing alone on top of the set of the *Tsimtsum*'s upper deck, which in turn was mounted on a gigantic gimbal, with an entire arsenal of special FX equipment pointed right at him. There were rain machines, wind machines capable of delivering gale-force gusts, air-pressurized water cannons that could knock you over with a blast of simulated ocean spray, and three 4,000-gallon dump tanks that could wash you overboard with the force of a giant wave. There was another machine pointing at Suraj as well, smaller than all of these, but, if anything, even more formidable and complicated: the 3-D camera.

The pressure to perform was intense, and Lee, who had taken Sharma practically by the hand through so many months of training, was far below, somewhere on the hangar

floor. To give any kind of direction, Lee would have to climb from one platform to another, and even then remain at a considerable distance from Sharma.

When second assistant director Ben Lanning yelled "action!" the gimbal kicked to life, pitching and rocking the set of the freighter. The rain started falling, the dump tanks unloading, the water cannons blasting, and the wind machines producing roaring, one-hundred-mile-per-hour gales. The entire cavernous hangar was periodically filled with flashes of bright, white light, freezing each artificial raindrop in midair. Sharma took a deep breath and . . .

"I didn't do anything," he says with a laugh. "I was so overwhelmed with the storm because to me, it *was* a storm. I was on this big ship and really high up, and it's moving crazily, and the rain is just hammering down, the wind's going crazy, and there's lightning—to me it was real." Tossed, heaved, pummeled, and thrown, Sharma, as he tells it, simply hung on. "I went through the action, but I didn't act," he says. "There were just so many things happening around me."

Lee had set the FX dial on high because this scene, after all, depicts the film's major storm; he was adamant that his actors react to real wind and the actual tilting of the deck. Sharma's sense of balance kicked in quickly enough and he was able to go through the motions of Pi dancing across the deck through the storm. In addition to these challenges, Sharma also needed to act in the sequence when Pi stops at the railing of the ship, suddenly realizes how steeply the *Tsimtsum* is tilting, and then sees a huge wave wash a couple of sailors overboard. "The choreography is the easier part for him, because he follows very well," says Lee. "But there's one thing, when he sees somebody get washed away, all of a sudden it sinks in he's in trouble. So that was acting. His face drops."

The distance imposed by the technical setup didn't make things easier. "Sometimes I would try just to let it rain, and scream to him during the shoot, forget about the sound," says Lee. The director would keep the camera rolling, making Sharma repeat part of the scene without cutting. "He looks, and he runs away. 'Come back!' And I give him directions, shouting it loud—'Blah, blah, blah, try it again. Action!'"

OPPOSITE TOP: *Suraj Sharma as Pi dances giddily in the storm.* OPPOSITE BOTTOM: *As he realizes something is wrong, he breaks into a run.* ABOVE: *Now the ship is tilting severely, and Pi watches in horror as a giant wave sweeps over the ship's lower decks.*

Though he had worked a lot with Sharma to lay the groundwork for Pi's character, Lee's approach to directing the actor in this situation seemed on the surface to be a lot of small, direct instructions of the "do-more-of-this-less-of-that" variety.

"It's not like the director says something magical, and then they act," says Lee. "Most of the time, it's very technical. It's like Thierry and his tiger," he continues, referring to the trainer Le Portier. "Only you and the tiger know that excitement. For everybody else watching you work, it'd be very boring. That's why I relate to Thierry so much. Except his act with the tiger is very immediate. If you miss by half a second, you're dead."

At the end of the day, Lee got the performance he wanted from his actor. The wind machines were turned off, the sprayers slowed to a dribble, the 75,000-pound *Tsimtsum* set was in precarious repose on top of the enormous gimbal. It was a wrap and tomorrow would be another day—day three of many, many more. There were no special words or gestures to mark Sharma's trial by water or a job pretty well done. Lee does not believe in showering young actors with too much praise, preferring just a few words of quiet encouragement: "I don't make

a big deal," he says. "It's their job. I always let them know they're so lucky to be in there. If you tell them don't screw up, they get nervous and that's not good either. Just tell them, always give a hundred percent, always be available and be in the best condition." And though Suraj Sharma still had a lot to learn, he had what would prove to be an unusual receptivity, which for Lee is the fundamental quality that defines a good actor.

A week later, having more or less gotten his simulated sea legs, Sharma got his first taste of performing his own stunts (which, it turned out, he could do quite well) when he was tossed over the side of the deck and into the lifeboat by the Taiwanese sailor extras. Hanging precariously off the *Tsimtsum*'s davits, the lifeboat was heavily weighted on one side by Sharma's fellow passenger, who had more than one hundred films with almost every great director of his time under his plus-size life-jacket, compared to Sharma's not-even-yet-one.

That passenger was Gérard Depardieu, who played the ship's French chef, a character who looms large in the second, "realistic" shipwreck story that Pi relates to the Japanese investigators at the end of the Martel novel. Since

this story is not actually shown in the film version, David Magee wrote a scene that established the chef as an on-screen presence: the Patel family go for their first meal in the *Tsimtsum*'s dingy cafeteria and are in for a rude and unappetizing surprise from the chef.

For five days, some of the focus was off Sharma as Depardieu filled the set with a mixture of Rabelaisian high spirits and consummate professionalism that captivated the cast and crew. "It was total fun, a blast," says Lee of working with Depardieu. "His continuity is all over the place but it's okay," the director continues. "Gérard is very easy to direct. He can do anything. 'Is it like this? Is it like that?' No method-acting garbage, just like—": Lee spreads his arms and makes a big, bull-in-a-china-shop crashing sound.

OPPOSITE TOP: *The sailors push Pi into the lifeboat, despite his protests that his family is still aboard.* OPPOSITE BOTTOM: *He may look as if he is praying, but Sharma is just checking his safety line.* ABOVE: *First-time actor Sharma finds himself sharing a boat with heavyweight veteran Gérard Depardieu.*

While the sinking of the *Tsimtsum* was physically demanding for Sharma, it didn't truly put his acting skills to the test. But that quickly changed, as the next stage in his journey as an actor was to play the teenage Pi at home in Pondicherry. There were no water cannons or hydraulic machinery for Sharma to face here—he needed to draw on some part of his old self, which he had left behind once he had been cast as Pi, and

would need to recover, with Lee's help. Though Sharma had arrived in Taiwan from his home in India only a few months prior, he had matured quickly after undergoing rigorous mental and physical training in pre-production.

"He had a few scenes [in India], like playing drums, chasing girls," says Lee. "He had to pretend he was dancing. And be a little goofy. There, it's a little challenging. Suraj was seventeen and now he looked like nineteen," Lee continues, "and [in India] he had to play like fifteen in order to look like sixteen." To accomplish this, the director drew on sense memory exercises that they had done together, for example: "Just remember what it's like physically when he's fourteen, fifteen," Lee says. At first Sharma's ability to revert would be associated with a specific memory from that period; with practice, it would become automatic. "I would remind him," says Lee. "Then it would become technical: 'You see, your eyes used to look that way. Your body's a little different.' And he'll remember those things. So next time he needs to get to that point he doesn't need to go all through the psychological memories."

SMALL PACKAGE, BIG BLAST

Twelve-year-old Ayush Tandon played Pi as a twelve-year-old—and he proved to be almost as formidable a presence on set and on screen as Depardieu. The Mumbai native, winner at age ten of the Indian dance reality TV show *Chhota Packet, Bada Dhamaka* (which can be translated as "Small Package, Big Blast") and star of more than fifty TV commercials, commanded the camera, earning the nickname "the one-taker" from costume designer Arjun Bhasin, who says: "He was so good that the other actors were nervous around him. Because they would do like three or four takes, and they'd finish a take and he'd say, 'Don't worry, start again.'" Lee agrees: "He was scary. He takes directions like an adult. It's like you can't believe he's twelve and when he plays, he plays like a twelve-year-old. He's uncanny."

OPPOSITE TOP: *Ang Lee demonstrates the art of brawling for the Tsimtsum's Taiwanese crew.* OPPOSITE BOTTOM: *Pi's father, Santosh (Adil Hussain), tries to teach the French chef (Gérard Depardieu) some manners.* LEFT: *Lee and Sharma in Pondicherry.*

A DANCER TAKES OFF ON THE RUNWAY

Shravanthi Sainath, a trained Bharatanatyam dancer, came to Taichung for a screen test for the part of Anandi, Pi's on-screen love interest. Afterward, she demonstrated some combinations of *adavus*, or dance movements, with *hastas*—the expressive hand gestures that Pi tries to imitate when he accosts Anandi outside the market—against a backdrop of tetrapods and heavy equipment for still photographer Phil Bray. Two weeks later in Pondicherry, Sainath danced as Anandi to Pi's faltering, smitten drumbeat.

india: empty zoos and crowded temples

While Lee and the Taiwan-based team had been busy testing the various technical waters, a large crew of four hundred plus was just finishing laying the groundwork for the upcoming Indian portion of the production, where locations from Pi's childhood, boyhood, and teenage years would be shot.

For many on set, the India shoot was one of the very best experiences in their professional lives. "It was all outside, and it's India in your face," says first assistant director (India) Nitya Mehra. "You were just shooting live constantly." The faded Gallic charm of Pondicherry and stunning natural beauty of Munnar were seductive. "You're always working out of cities like Mumbai and Delhi, which are anywhere," says Mehra, speaking for the Indian crew. "So when we were there, we were like, let's just not bang it in with cars, everything. Everyone got cycles, because the distance is not too much. On that note, it was a lot of fun."

TOP: *Lee and director of photography Claudio Miranda shoot a close-up of Anandi (Shravanthi Sainath) tying a rakhi thread around Pi's wrist in their farewell scene under the Pondicherry pier.* ABOVE: *Lee and associate producer Michael Malone receive blessings on the first day of the India shoot.*

TOP: Sadhus—wandering holy men who have given up all material attachments (although nothing prevents them from being movie extras).

ABOVE LEFT: A mother and her daughters, extras at the Marché Goubert, Pondicherry's central market.

RIGHT: An extra among marigold garlands at the flower market.

A genuine enchantment seemed to hover over the shoot, but one that would not have been possible without the long preparation put in by line producer (India) Tabrez Noorani (*Slumdog Millionaire; Eat, Pray, Love*), Mehra, and their large crew. They set up a filmmaking infrastructure in places there were none, secured the sorts of locations (a mosque, a thousand-year-old temple) where cameras normally never go, negotiated with officials over countless cups of chai, and kept all noise and distractions at arm's length so that Lee could get his shots done and only hear about what happened afterward, in the form of stories rather than as urgent news bulletins.

Though the first act of *Life of Pi* passes by on screen as a series of charming vignettes of coming of age, it was, according to Noorani, "probably the largest set up that India has seen in terms of foreign film. I mean, the infrastructure was larger than the *Gandhi* infrastructure." It was an epic preparation for an intimate scale. The main reason for this was that Pondicherry and Munnar were not places that were geared toward filmmaking. "It's impossible to shoot in Pondicherry with forty people," says Noorani, "and we were three hundred plus. Moving a hundred cars and fifty trucks in that city, you can't really do that because the city is tripled. You can't move anything during the day, which means that you can't move locations during the day. So you have to set up a second unit that all they did was, they'd move at night. But that was the fun part about it. For me, that's why I end up on certain projects—I mean, if there's no challenge, what's the fun?"

"We just had to start from scratch," says Mehra, who worked with a large crew of extras, coordinators, and assistants. Mehra says that second assistant directors Rob Burgess and Ben Lanning made fun of her, saying "Are you making *Ben Hur* in India, that so you have so many assistants?" But the extras were not professionals; they were mostly people "literally pulled off the streets," with absolutely no conception of what it meant to be part of a production. Whether it was putting in a few passers-by on the street, ornamenting a tea field in Munnar with four hundred brightly dressed tea pickers, or emptying seven villages to get the 1,500 extras needed for the big temple festival sequence, these people needed to be found and trained—a task that required skill, sensitivity, diplomacy, and sometimes a bit of show biz.

THE PONDICHERRY ALBUM

These photos, taken during scouting trips, give a flavor of Pondicherry, the most important remaining French outpost in India after the country's colonial ambitions on the subcontinent were definitively crushed by the British in the mid-eighteenth century. The older districts of town still have a strong French flavor, with their tidy gridded street layout, French-style villas, street signs, and policemen in kepis.

among schoolchildren

Take, for example, all the schoolchildren that were needed for the sequence in which Piscine Molitor Patel, tired of the urinary puns at the expense of his odd, swimming-pool inspired name, transforms himself into "Pi." Over the older Pi's narration at the beginning of the film, we see a quick succession of scenes involving crowds of mocking, jostling schoolboys, a very determined twelve-year-old with a piece of chalk, a series of blackboards, and an irrational number that goes on and on until the jeering is replace by cheering when Pi triumphantly assumes his new identity.

"We needed different kids, age groups, and everything," says Mehra. "And so we had to pull them out of school. And then we would take them into the soccer field, and I would train them the way I trained the extras. You know, about how you can't look into the camera. And sure enough, once that big giant camera's there, you know, they weren't going to listen much to it. But it was super fun," adds Mehra. "The younger boys were beautiful." Following Lee's ideas, costume designer Arjun Bhasin did not make twelve-year-old Pi stand out from the rest of the schoolchildren in any way. "I went to those kind of schools when I was little," says the now quite dapper Bhasin, "where you weren't allowed to wear anything that everyone else wasn't wearing. I mean, not a watch or a pair of shoes. And then Pi realizes that he is special. Nobody is like everybody else." Though Pi's true individuality comes as part of his journey on the boat years later, the realization probably dawns at the age of twelve, when he separates himself from his name by an act of theater on the school blackboard, and then goes through repeated attempts at transformation as he tries on one religious faith after another.

OPPOSITE TOP: Je m'appelle π: Piscine Molitor Patel writes his new name on the blackboard in French class.
OPPOSITE BOTTOM: Ang Lee and Ayush Tandon (as twelve-year-old Pi) in the classroom.
ABOVE: Lee and first assistant director (India) Nitya Mehra, trying to make an unruly roomful of extras laugh on cue.
LEFT: The bulky 3-D camera doesn't lend itself to hand-held work, but cameraman Lukasz Bielen gives it a good shot.

three places of worship and two kinds of trouble

Having been introduced to God in his manifold aspects through the Hindu faith into which he was born, Pi's religious curiosity blossoms as he grows older, leading him to further religious explorations where he discovers Christ and Allah. For this part of the story, the production was fortunate to secure access to three of the most authentic and beautiful places of worship in and near Pondicherry.

The Church

The first and last locations to be shot in the India trip—the interior of the Holy Rosary Church in Pondicherry and exterior shots of the mountainous tea-growing station of Munnar in the neighboring state of Kerala—were combined to form the sequence in which Pi discovers Christianity. The exterior shots required a great deal of setting up. "In Munnar, for example, the shots we were taking were very simple," says Mehra. "But the thing is with Ang—I love that about him, about his scale—you know, he'd just point, and he'd be like, 'Nitya, do you think we can get, you know, some tea pickers on that mountain?' Now, that mountain, just to get there, in Munnar, takes forty-five minutes." And Lee wanted not just a few tea pickers, but four or five hundred at a time, which meant finding and training up to nine hundred extras who had to be dressed in layers of bright prints and colors. Like the placement of small figures in a Chinese landscape painting, the tea pickers moving across the vast landscape add an element of fleeting, almost intimate beauty.

ABOVE: *Tea pickers, Munnar: "We wanted color, and Ang wanted it to be like prints and busy and layers," says costume designer Arjun Bhasin, who dressed more than eight hundred extras.* OPPOSITE TOP: *Tea plantations, Munnar, Kerala, overlooking the neighboring state of Tamil Nadu.* OPPOSITE BOTTOM: *Ang Lee directs Ayush Tandon to sneak into the church where Pi discusses Christ with the priest (Andrea Stephano).*

The Mosque

To shoot in Pondicherry's Jamia Mosque, a graceful, white-washed building in the city's small Muslim quarter, was a challenge even for Noorani, who in the past had obtained permission to film in New Delhi's largest mosque. Finally, everything was cleared and exceptional permission to shoot inside was granted, but only within certain parameters, the most important of which was that the camera could not go inside the mosque beyond a certain point within the building; a blue screen was placed on the threshold, and the crowd inside was added later, in post-production. Noorani had been

careful to cultivate a personal relationship with the imam— "the minute anyone wants to shoot in India, I feel that's the most important thing," he says. "They're all educated people. So the imam knows about Ang. He loved the fact that Ang was just so—Ang was Ang. He was simple, humble, and he chatted with him. I think that made a big difference."

The Hindu Temple

The Sri Gokilambal Thirukameshwara Hindu Temple is located in Villianur, about six miles away from Pondicherry. It had never been used for a film and, with elements dating back to the twelfth century, was much older than the average temple used as a backdrop for musical numbers in Bollywood productions.

To represent the magical quality of Hinduism in the life of Pi (in this case, his five-year-old self, played by Gautham Belur), Lee decided to stage a temple float festival in honor of Vishnu, with hundreds of worshippers and the glittering light of thousands of floating clay oil lamps, or *diyas*—a dazzling spectacle.

Lee based the idea of the floating Vishnu on an image and a description of a float festival that was discovered in the early stages of research. In this type of festival, an image of the deity is brought out, often at night, and floated around

the central basin, or tank, of the temple. On board the raft are Brahmin priests as well as musicians playing for the deity, while worshippers throng the sides of the tank. The local priests had no particular model for such a festival at Villianur, but certain elements such as the *diyas* and ritual gestures were nearly always observed in such situations. "It's that faith that I find so fantastic about our country," Mehra explains. "The thirty-million-gods multiplicity of Hinduism is such that this ceremony could be both a complete invention and, at the same time, deeply authentic."

The feeling of authenticity comes in part from the large throng of extras, the entire populations of a number of local villages recruited for that one scene. Earlier, Mehra and her assistants had done a rehearsal with seven hundred of them, to teach them the language of film: what "action" meant, what "cut" meant, and exactly where to go when she said "back to one." "The villagers just stood around, and they loved it," says Mehra. "They were laughing at us, because they were just like, what are these crazy people doing? And I said, 'Now go and tell the other villagers what a blast you had.'"

Because of the digital camera's sensitivity to low light, most of the actors and extras in the float festival segment were lit by candlelight, with the artificial lights mainly illuminating the temple backgrounds. Everyone in the production participated in lighting the lamps and launching them across the water. With about three thousand floating lights in the water, and another three thousand scattered across the grounds, the effect was incredible. Kho Shin Wong, David Womark's assistant, says, "The process was almost like more than just the filming of a movie. In the way that Ang embodies the entire movie all the time, we were able to help embody that aspect of it. And it's what helped bring the crew closer together, too." "It was a very, very exciting night. Nothing like it, very spiritual," says Lee, recalling how the wind blew strong that night. "All night long the crew kept lighting candles." Makeup and hair designer Fae Hammond, who has worked and traveled in India a number of times, said, "For me, that was my most magical moment of filmmaking—ever. It was like we were just India'd out. Just relaxed—and the imagery was incredible."

OPPOSITE TOP: *Pi catches a glimpse of Muslim women praying.*
OPPOSITE BOTTOM: *Pi stands outside the gates of the mosque.*
ABOVE: *The Sri Gokilambal Thirukameshwara Hindu temple in Villanur, near Pondicherry. Parts of the temple date back to the thirteenth century.*

"You know what makes Ang so special? He sees the largeness of the thing. Mostly when foreign crews come to India, they want elephants and bright things, dance girls, swirling. They want that exotic-y India: peacocks and saris. And Ang only wanted that to show the isolation of the boy later—to contrast the two things. He doesn't show off."

—ARJUN BASIN, COSTUME DESIGNER

TOP: Up late: five-year-old Pi (Gautam Belur, left) and his older brother Ravi (Ayaan Khan) bask in the glow of the temple ceremony in the company of their skeptical father (Adil Hussain). ABOVE: On the float, the statue of Vishnu reclining on a bed of snakes, with his consort Lakshmi, is attended by Brahmin priests, while musicians play the nadaswaram—a South Indian woodwind. RIGHT: Extras lighting oil lamps for the float festival scene.

Producer Gil Netter concurs, calling that night "probably one of my all-time favorite memories of any movie I've ever worked on."

For all the spectacle, there's an intimate human dimension to the scene. "Actually, when you see the scene, it's about this little boy," says Arjun Bhasin. "And I think, if I had that skill of understanding the gist of what that moment is, rather than getting lost in the beauty and the size and the scale of it, I would be so successful in my life. And so I learned that. I loved being able to see India through that kind of light."

zoo stories

In the end, there was an overabundance of extras in some of the Indian location scenes. But getting animals to fill the set of the Pondicherry Zoo was a more challenging proposition. India's animal protection laws, particularly as they relate to the use of animals in film, are among the most stringent in the world. Large animals could not be transported from other zoos, but it was possible to secure an assortment of smaller creatures—rabbits, goats, birds— plus an elephant for the set. The rest of the animals were filmed at Taiwanese zoos and, along with a few computer-generated creatures, added in post-production.

The Bengal tigers were born, raised, and trained in France and Canada and filmed on the set in Taichung.

OPPOSITE TOP: A stand-in for the giraffe that would be digitally inserted later on.
OPPOSITE BOTTOM: On the monitor, Pi's mother (Tabu) tends the plants in the botanical garden.
ABOVE: Pi shows off Richard Parker to Anandi. (The reverse shot of the actual tiger exhibit was filmed in Taiwan.) LEFT: Production designer David Gropman discusses details of the zoo with Ang Lee.

the journey: production   107

FOUR TIGERS AND A HYENA

Let's meet the four real-life felines and one hyena who made their contributions to the role of Pi's fellow traveler. Needless to say, the process of filming tigers wasn't as linear and predictable as shooting with a human actor. As David Ticotin, whose unit spent the most time with King and company, observes: "the one thing you have to remember when working with animals is that every day is different. Every minute is different. So we just keep rolling the camera." He adds, "We have to."

But in the end, each tiger contributed his or her share of moments that would become part of Richard Parker's performance. As the main model for Richard Parker, King was used a great deal for close-ups, more than any of the other tigers. Along with providing extensive, detailed reference footage for the animators in post-production, the other tigers had some fine on-screen moments as well.

OPPOSITE: **King** is described by his trainer, Thierry Le Portier, as "very intelligent," and "the most beautiful"—a tiger's tiger.

ABOVE: **Minh**, King's beautiful sister, is "calm and cool," according to Le Portier, but with a bold side that came out in front of the cameras.

TOP RIGHT: **Themis**, looking fierce, was in fact quite a professional, whose previous credits include Two Brothers.

CENTER RIGHT: Described by the crew members as a "pussycat," **Jonas**, the fourth tiger, came with his trainer, Niall Higgins, from Canada.

RIGHT: Along with the felines, Le Portier also brought **Vlad**, a spotted hyena, one of seven that he owns, to the set. By the end of the shoot Vlad and Lee had become fast friends: "I love the hyena," Lee says. "She let me scratch her neck, she made a noise—a crazy, shrieking noise. I think I'm the only one she let do that other than the trainer."

shooting tigers in taichung

After the India portion of the shoot, *Life of Pi* became two parallel productions, with a second splinter unit in Taiwan under the direction of first assistant director David Ticotin shooting the animals' routines and reactions for various specific scenes that were being shot with Sharma in the main tank. (The two co-stars of *Life of Pi* could never share the same space, except digitally.) "Each one of the shots had to cut into a sequence that Ang had designed," says Ticotin. Which translated to a lot of shots.

While the tiger trainers rehearsed the animals, a team led by visual effects supervisor Bill Westenhofer and VFX producer Susan MacLeod observed and videotaped the sessions, ultimately creating an entire library of tiger details: the way a tiger's paws compress on the ground as it walks, the way the animal stretches and yawns, the way the skin on a tiger's belly (which hangs slightly loose, like a house cat's) swings back and forth as the animal saunters away—all of which served as raw material when it was time to construct the digital elements of Richard Parker in post-production.

piscine molitor

As work with the tigers continued, a large-scale replica of a celebrated Parisian Art Deco swimming pool rose out of the tarmac next door: the Piscine Molitor. The pretext, of course, was a brief scene shot to accompany the adult Pi's narration of how he got his name, Piscine Molitor Patel, thanks to his *mamaji* ("honorary uncle"), who venerated the pool as the purest and most beautiful in the world. And so on an unseasonably cold March day, 120 extras, dressed as sun-worshipping 1950s Parisians—all bright red lipstick and frilly pastel bikinis—arrived in Taichung to start work.

While costume designer Arjun Bhasin had kept things plain for the Pondicherry scenes, he allowed himself a lot more leeway with the swimming pool sequence. He and production designer David Gropman worked together to create a very particular color palette, bringing out a kind of artificiality without violating historical authenticity.

OPPOSITE: *Themis is ready for her close-up.* TOP: *Jonas, finding his inner housecat. The action was filmed for the scene where Richard Parker swats at a swarm of flying fish.* ABOVE: *Mamaji, Pi's honorary uncle, swimming through the pure waters of the Piscine Molitor.*

ABOVE: The Piscine Molitor, circa 1950, as imagined by the art department, with the help of old postcards. RIGHT: The set of the Piscine Molitor. OPPOSITE LEFT: Crowd assistant director Katie Lee doggedly scoured Taichung for European extras with flyers and footwork. OPPOSITE RIGHT: A list of requirements for extras, from flip-flops to makeup.

Casting Call
for *Life of Pi*

We are looking for **European**-look extras
for our retro Parisian pool scene.

If you have your friends and family here,
and they might be interested in being part of this retro scene,
you are more than welcome to contact Katie Lee

Pool Party!   Life of Pi

The Memo
[Let's rock the show.]
The shooting is scheduled for 2 days: March 3rd (Thursday) and March 14th (Monday).

Please bring along the following items:

1. **A (water-proof) coat / robe / beach towel**: to keep warm or to protect from the sun, while on set waiting. (Be aware some might be painted over to reinforce the skin tone. Please bring something **inexpensive**.)

2. **Slippers / sandals / flip-flops**: to walk around comfortably on set

3. For ladies, please come WITHOUT makeup and please wear your **TOEnails** "red red." (No need to worry about your FINGERnails. The makeup artists will take care of that.)

"It's kind of fantastical, but it's not," says Bhasin about the dreamlike quality of the costumes and set. "There's so much about it like a story being told to Pi as a child, who's then telling the story to somebody else, and it's like Chinese whispers [the game of telephone], you know? When you get to the end of it and you see it visually, it's like, is that really what happened? Or is it someone's interpretation of someone's interpretation of someone's interpretation of what that could have been?"

Like the Temple float festival—indeed, like all of *Life of Pi*—the entire world that Lee built up exists only in order to frame a small figure. Here, Mamaji, Pi's swimming guru and pool connoisseur (played by Elias Alouf, Sharma's yoga coach), stands solemnly poised as if on the edge of some holy river, about to dive in. When he does, the Piscine Molitor's liquid, enhanced by 3-D, shimmers and ripples so pristinely that for a brief moment, Mamaji's assertion that this swimming pool's water is so pure that it can cleanse the soul seems not so absurd after all.

ABOVE: *The Piscine Molitor in 2009. The pool was abandoned to graffiti for years, though plans are afoot to transform it into a new sports complex.* TOP RIGHT: *Pi faces Mecca.* BOTTOM: *During a break, Tabu leans against Vibish Sivikumar, who plays her son and sixteen-year-old Pi's older brother Ravi, while Adil Hussain discusses the scene with the director.* OPPOSITE TOP: *Ang Lee and Tabu work on Pi's mother's kolam. The geometrical patterns, made of rice flour, ornament the thresholds of many South Indian homes, welcoming visitors, bringing prosperity, and protecting against evil spirits.* OPPOSITE BOTTOM: *Twelve-year-old Pi says grace before supper.*

pi's home away from india

On February 11, 2011, the crew and Indian cast returned to Taichung, where Pi's home life was shot on a soundstage. Pi's childhood home is the setting for Pi at three different stages of his life and three stages of faith. Six days later, with the domestic scenes completed, the Patel household was shuttered. India, both real and constructed, was left behind for good. A brief scene of farewell to India on the *Tsimtsum* deck, followed by another moment in the cargo hold sealed shut the movie's first act, its "past." Five days later, Sharma was in the water. As definitively as Pi departs from home, the production had moved into a new phase.

pi's life, suraj's journey

In the beginning of production, Suraj Sharma had other actors—both older and more experienced—to react to, to share the camera with, to ease the pressure. Now they were gone. So was the vibrancy of India: the temples, the candles, the mountains, the colors. Sharma was alone, on a raft or on a boat, in a wave tank or on gimbals, surrounded by a horizonless, artificial blue. He was left with Richard Parker—who, when not completely absent from the set, was represented by a variety of more-or-less tiger-shaped objects that were put there as placeholders (along with other creature substitutes).

How does someone spend day after day acting opposite nothing? Lee maintains that it's not impossible. "If they're talented, anybody can do it," he says. He had Sharma spend some time observing the real tigers, but for the most part, the director believes, "Acting is pretending. Pure. You can borrow experience or whatever, but the final result is what matters. It's really about how much the audience believes. Of course, if you have the actors believing and the filmmakers believing, it's a good step in between. But it's not equivalent to the final result. So I don't buy that, to act something for real you have to experience it."

Even so, Sharma couldn't help feeling as if he had stepped into a completely different movie. "In India, I was reacting to other people, so that made it a little easier for me," he says. "I didn't have to imagine things. There was actually something there that had expressions and I could react to those expressions."

Now, like Pi himself, Sharma was alone.

trial by water

Alone, but not entirely adrift, Sharma had learned to swim. He had learned to dive. He had trained and prepared and watched and listened. He quickly picked up a sense of each department and how they fit together. "He helped. He reset his props," says script supervisor Mary Cybulski. "He helped guys move apartments. He was a film worker like the rest of us." And though his time with *daoyan*—the respectful Chinese form of address for "director" and what Sharma called Lee—was often limited to one or two minutes before the cameras rolled, he had internalized much of what Lee had taught him during their one-on-one meetings in pre-production.

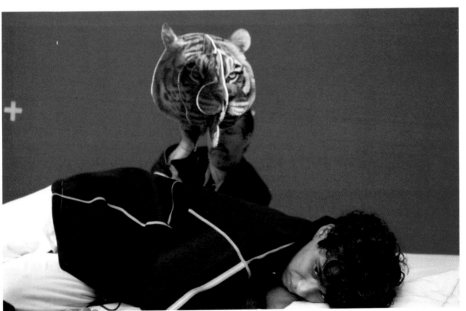

OPPOSITE: *Leaving Pondi: Lee and Sharma contemplate the production's transition from India to the Pacific.* ABOVE: *A final view of the Patel zoo in the Tsimtsum cargo hold.* LEFT: *The mock-up of Richard Parker's head helps the camera frame the shot to include the computer-generated tiger that will be added in post-production.*

"In the beginning it was scary: I was scared of water," Sharma admits. "But I just started trying not to see the blue screen but to see the ocean and whatever Pi sees."

Pi Patel and Suraj Sharma's stories ran parallel to each other in a rising arc at first; as Pi starts off by mastering his physical environment, so Sharma drew upon the months of physical training that he underwent with stunt coordinator Charlie Croughwell and Croughwell's son, Cameron. Though it wasn't a foregone conclusion, from the beginning, Lee preferred that Sharma do as many of the stunts himself as possible rather than use stunt doubles. This was partly a consequence of 3-D—or at least Lee's vision of 3-D, which favored long takes and a relatively still camera over a lot of movement and cutting. "Ang feels the 3-D experience should not be broken up by a lot of camera angles," explains William Connor. "That once you're in it you should stay in it, without too much coverage." So the opportunities to cut between Sharma and a long shot, say, or the back of a stunt double's head were few and far between.

That said, Sharma's safety could not be compromised. The fact that he didn't get sick after being soaked outdoors nearly every day during an unseasonably cold spring was a miracle.

Not getting injured during stunts, on the other hand, was a matter of very careful preparation. "You have to figure out the gag," says Charlie Croughwell, using the tech word for "stunt." "You always test the gag before you perform it with the actor." Croughwell used his son Cameron for this purpose. "There was a thing where we needed a wave to pick Suraj up and slam him on top of the boat," says Croughwell. "He needs to ride this wave. We figure out the mechanics with Cameron, then we take Suraj's double, Nikeeth Thomas, and put him in after we've worked out the most difficult part of it; then test it with him, and let Suraj watch it. We get Suraj out in the water, out in the waves; you have to just work your way up to this, but he's more than competent, more than capable of doing all his own stunts."

Though the actor's movement was controlled by wires, the waves were also on full force. Even artificially generated waves can be unpredictable—in fact, they were meant to be, up to a point, for the sake of realism. Sharma's natural abilities, reinforced by training and the full support of Croughwell's back-up team, were in evidence from early on. The young actor's combination of intense discipline and good-natured willingness to try anything that won the day. "When they start the effects, I have three seconds of lots of fun every time," says Sharma, "with all the rain and storms . . . actually it's fun."

Another *Tsimtsum*-sinking-related stunt, which seemed to faze onlookers from the crew more than the performer himself, was the so-called barrel roll. The stunt was done during the sinking of the *Tsimtsum* storm, and the lifeboat was required to pop out of the water and roll over, with Pi clinging to it. This particular stunt illustrates the importance of timing in water.

The boat was hung on hooks and lowered upside down into the water with Suraj Sharma attached to the tarp (and a breathing apparatus nearby); then it was lifted right above the water, and held there, still upside down as the waves rose and fell, alternately engulfing the actor, while Lee and Croughwell watched. "Watching the waves goes before lighting," says the director, "before which camera to use. You observe the water first. You can't do it backwards or you might waste three hours. You really have to know the water." Lee waited for a wave that he liked, then called "action"; after this, Croughwell waited for the moment when the water was at its lowest for the stunt to work properly. When he gave the signal, the boat was dropped into the trough of a wave and, with the help of specially designed holes, popped out of the water and rolled over, revealing Sharma, no longer strapped on, looking like he was clinging to the craft for dear life.

In Croughwell's experience, doing stunts is not just about the physical training: "You have a particular talent for stunts. You either can do it or you can't. Suraj does have the talent, definitely, he has great timing, he's very coordinated.

OPPOSITE: *The wave lift stunt: a swell lifts Suraj Sharma up and, with the help of a wire, slams him down on top of the lifeboat.* THIS PAGE, TOP TO BOTTOM: *The barrel-roll stunt: 1) The boat is held upside down, with Sharma waiting underneath; 2) Lee yells "action," and the boat is dropped down into the water. The boat pops up again and; 3) rolls over, with Sharma clinging precariously to the side; 4) It's time for a break.*

He started out with a natural inclination, he just didn't know he had it in him."

According to Croughwell, the most difficult stunts in the film for Sharma were the deep tank dives, which were part of the *Tsimtsum* sequence (though they were actually shot much later). There's a scene at the very beginning of the *Tsimtsum* sinking sequence where Pi swims down the flooded corridor—a sixty-foot-long set in the deep-water tank inside one of the hangars—in search of his parents. And shortly afterward, there's a brief interlude of unbearable loss in the midst of the raging storm in which Pi hovers, suspended under the surface, watching the freighter sink.

"Those two scenes in particular, it's a long breath hold," says Croughwell, who worked with Sharma to increase the actor's lung capacity. "He had to have incredible control underwater as well. He had to be able to swim down, no mask on, no goggles. He had to be able to stop in a very specific spot and understand the dynamics of buoyancy control and just hover there, and then be able to swim back up in exactly the same direction that we specified and at the same time avoid getting bumped by a shark and all these other elements. If he could do those things, he could do anything."

And he did.

TOP: *Sharma prepares for Pi's plunge.* CENTER: *Pi swims down sixty feet of flooded Tsimtsum corridors in search of his parents.* BOTTOM: *Suraj Sharma hovers underwater in one of the most challenging stunts of the shoot, which involved complex choreography and long breath holding.*

SURAJ SHARMA: THE HARDEST-WORKING MAN IN SHOW BUSINESS

Individually, each of these production stills represents a dramatic moment in the film—usually Pi making a quick getaway from Richard Parker or getting knocked sideways by a storm swell. But put all the photos together on one page—and imagine how many more of them there are, and then imagine how many more leaps went undocumented by the still photographers— and something of both the heroic and comic dimensions of Suraj Sharma's work begins to emerge. Even with an extensive support system and backup, simply falling into the water was not without its hazards. But that's what Sharma did, scene after scene, again and again, in every possible way.

SHAKEN AND STIRRED: MAKE MINE A GIMBAL

For almost every major sequence filmed in the wave tank, certain shots were also filmed on lifeboats affixed to the top of gimbals, which, unlike even the most sophisticated wave tank, could be programmed with a repeatable set of motions when a close-up was required—for example, when Pi, clinging to the oar, having just seen the *Tsimtsum* go down, cries out for his family. A gimbal might also be needed if there was a particularly complicated shot that required precise choreography, as in the first minutes after the lifeboat detaches from the sinking freighter and spins across the waves at high speed (done with a combination of the big gimbal with an added rotator on top, plus the Spydercam).

Aside from the big gimbal, there were also smaller-sized units for light motion, manual control, and work with the tigers throughout the shoot. Then there was the "rotisserie" boat—so-called because it rotated back and forth on an axis—a sadistic contraption specially created by the SFX department for the Storm of God sequence, where Pi retreats under the boat's tarp with Richard Parker to wait out the worst of the weather. The effect, plainly visible on the video feed during the shoot, was like watching a person go through the heavy-duty wash cycle at the laundromat.

LEFT: *Setting up for a close-up of Pi, the morning after the sinking of the Tsimtsum.* BELOW: *Pi watches the Tsimtsum sink, taking everything he has ever known with it.* OPPOSITE TOP LEFT: *Part of the Storm of God sequence, shot on a gimbal. There's an enormous dump tank full of water behind Suraj Sharma. Wait for it . . .* OPPOSITE TOP RIGHT: *. . . and here it comes! The gimbal operator is in the foreground. Though the sequence is largely pre-programmed, he can make adjustments with the steering mechanism.* OPPOSITE BOTTOM: *The "rotisserie" in action for the Storm of God sequence: as the boat rotated around, Sharma would often become completely submerged.*

Until a few scenes before the Storm of God, Pi's journey is a very physical and intuitive one: he's in survival mode, mastering his environment and the tiger. "He's getting good, and starting to get comfortable," says Lee—talking about both the character of Pi and the increasingly confident professional playing him. But it is the Storm of God, the pendant to the storm that sinks the *Tsimtsum* that marks a moment of transition in Pi's journey. In many ways that scene in the film marked another step in Sharma's transformation, a transformation partly managed by the director. A more spiritual dimension enters into the film, a dissolution of the self into the surrounding vast unknown that Lee wanted Sharma to access.

"It wasn't about the physical anymore. And I wanted the look in his eyes to be very spiritual." Lee made playlists for Sharma's iPod of what became known as "spooky God music"—mostly choral, ranging from Gregorian chants to the avant-garde *Requiem* by the Hungarian composer György Ligeti that Stanley Kubrick used so effectively in *2001*. "I started talking philosophy and religion with him," says Lee. "One thing that worked for him is that I asked him to start praying every night. He has to kneel down by the bed. But he doesn't pray to any god—he just designates something that works for him—speaks to that person and confesses." Yoga also went back into the mix. "And," adds Lee, "I asked him not to talk to anyone, as much as he could. And I told people, don't bother him. Just leave him alone."

BELOW: *Suraj Sharma's face on the monitor captures Pi's increasing disconnection from reality.* OPPOSITE: *Pi, adrift.*

"In this part of the movie, the storm part, there's a lot of acting, but a lot of it is also survival—which, somehow, everyone has in them."
—SURAJ SHARMA

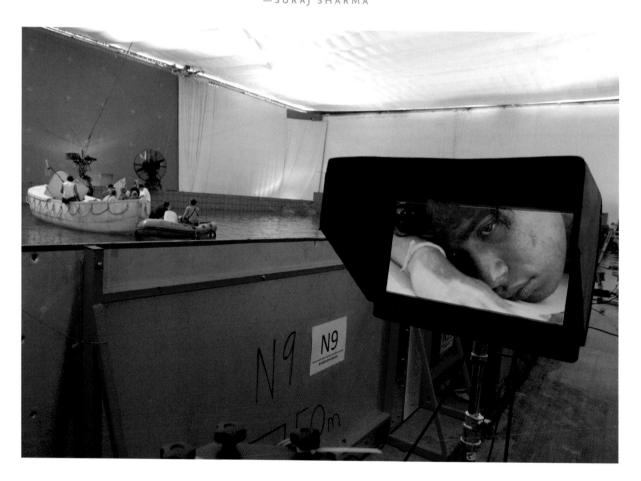

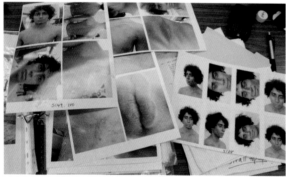

All of this was by way of keeping Sharma in character, to prepare him for the two most emotionally difficult scenes in the film: above all, the Mexican infirmary scene at the very end, of course—the long, challenging monologue that got Sharma the part of Pi in the first place. And leading up to that, and in some ways just as important—at least as a stage in the acting journey that would help Sharma prepare for the Mexican infirmary scene—was the scene after the Storm of God when Pi believes that he and Richard Parker are dying. He has to cry on cue. For Sharma, the emotional challenge

was of a different magnitude than the physical feats he had accomplished so far.

The scheduled beach landing having been rained out, the scene was shot with the sketchiest of sets: the lifeboat against a portable blue screen under the roof of a school bus depot in a small provincial town in southern Taiwan. "I was sort of apologetic about this not being the right conditions," says Lee, "but by that time, Suraj was now a pretty serious actor. So it's 'I've gotta do this.'"

He found Sharma looking rather despondent. "I went up to him and I said, 'So this is what we're going to do. It's going to be okay.' He told me he wasn't in that place."

"I kept trying to push these sad thoughts in my head and think of all the things we'd been through and about how everything is suddenly coming to an end, " says Sharma. "But I was still not able to cry."

Lee called "Cut" and took Sharma aside. "His character, Pi, is crying with depth; with what he went through in that journey, all that he lost, with fatigue—all these layers of sorrow." So, as Lee puts it, "I gave him a layer." He started with basic sorrow, telling the actor: "You and the tiger are dying." Sharma

tried the take again. "Better, but not quite there yet," Lee said, and then he gave Sharma another layer: "You and the tiger are dying, and you have lost everything." Another take, another layer: "The final layer was fatigue," Lee recalls. "The description of acting is really abstract. You can only be so specific. At some point you've got to describe what to do in terms of body function: It's natural. It's fatigue." That's what he told Sharma: "You and the tiger are dying; and you have lost everything; and you are tired, so tired, and physically numb."

The cameras rolled, and Sharma cried.

Script supervisor Mary Cybulski was stunned. "Suraj really gave himself over to Ang," she says. "He cried in a really surrendering way that most high school guys just can't bring themselves to do, that most grown-up actors can't bring themselves to do." Says Lee: "Suraj has to work through all the layers of numbness, physical numbness, to reach that deep kind of emotion—he's not just crying tears—this makes a big difference."

"And it was quite brilliant. And the third take, it was just like everybody's heart . . ." Lee pauses. "I was very proud of Suraj."

And he told him so.

OPPOSITE TOP: Lee and makeup designer Fae Hammond put on the final touches. OPPOSITE BOTTOM: From the makeup department's ring binder, the late-stage "look" of Pi's journey. TOP: The director and his actor. ABOVE: How to cradle a dying tiger: Lee blocks the scene for Sharma.

"Suraj became a kind of spiritual leader to all of us. Seeing him go about trying his best, not getting sick, not getting hurt. Everything he does is genuine, because it's his first time. Crews appreciate that kind of actor. It just reminds everybody why they want to be filmmakers."

—ANG LEE

TOP: "We're dying, Richard Parker." The tiger's weakness allows the one moment of physical contact between the boy and the animal. ABOVE: The blue "stuffie" has been digitally replaced.

a passage to india: a portfolio by mary ellen mark

Photographer Mary Ellen Mark has produced many iconic cinematic portraits, collected in her book *Seen Behind the Scenes: Forty Years of Photographing on Set*—the calligraphic curve of Federico Fellini's stocky frame as he calls out through the bullhorn on the set of *Satyricon*; or Marlon Brando, a giant beetle punctuating his shaved head, staring up at the viewer with dark Kurtzian irony from the heart of Francis Ford Coppola's *Apocalypse Now*. But the larger part of Mark's career has been devoted to photo essays on the marginalized, the exploited, and the eccentric: residents of a women's psychiatric ward, street kids in Portland, prostitutes in Bombay (Mumbai). The latter were the subjects of her book *Falkland Road*, one of the earliest fruits of a long relationship with India that also inspired her to produce work on the Indian circus and street performers.

This combination of background and sensibility made Mark a great fit for capturing the India section of the *Life of Pi* shoot. She also returned at the end of production to catch a few days of filming scenes in and around the

beach resort of Kenting, which included Pi's farewell to Richard Parker and his landing in Mexico. Complementing the work of still photographers Phil Bray, Peter Sorel, and Jake Netter, Mark brought an old-school vision to the set. In a world gone digital, she remains stubbornly analog, enamored of working in black and white, chasing light with her beaten-up Leicas, and capturing slivers of her subjects' souls on the silver emulsion of old-fashioned film.

ABOVE: *Photographer Mary Ellen Mark with extras for the mosque scene.*

LEFT: *"He's so expressive, if he'd only take off those hats."* —Mary Ellen Mark.

OPPOSITE TOP LEFT: Adil Hussain, who plays Santosh Patel (Pi's father).
OPPOSITE TOP RIGHT: Shravanthi Sainath as Anandi, the Bharatanatyam
dancer who captures Pi's heart. OPPOSITE BOTTOM: Tabu, who plays Gita
Patel (Pi's mother). TOP AND ABOVE LEFT: Ayush Tandon, as twelve-year-

ABOVE: The domino
effect: schoolboy extras
kick back between takes.
RIGHT: Men from
Pondicherry's Muslim
quarter waiting in the
extras holding area
OPPOSITE: Suraj
Sharma, at rest

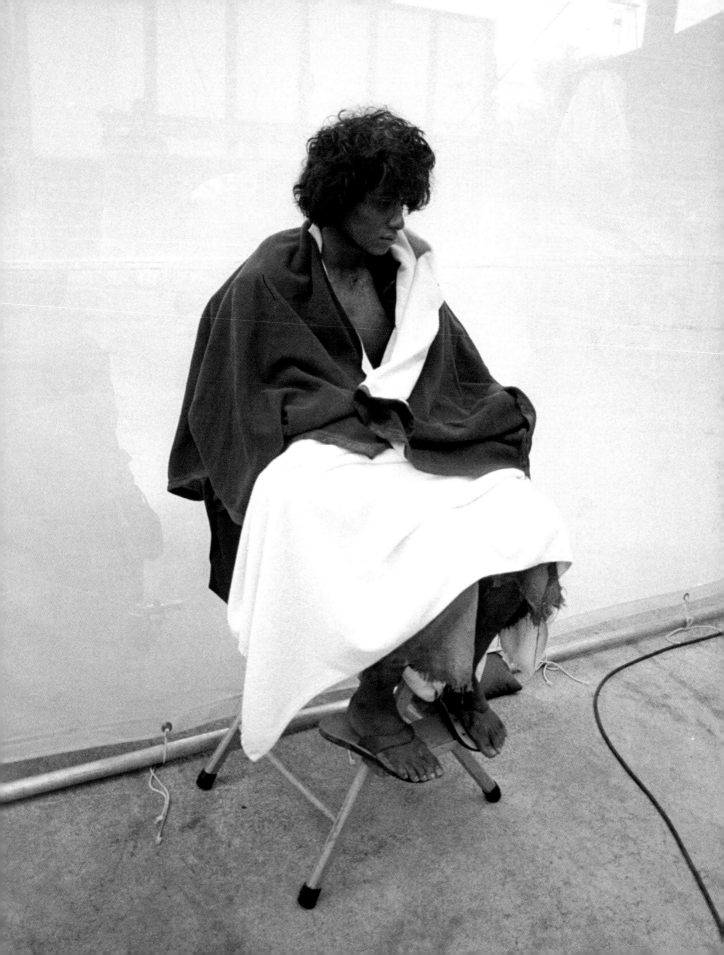

4 reaching shore: post-production

On a brisk winter afternoon, Ang Lee—along with visual effects producer Susan MacLeod and editor Tim Squyres—was sitting in the comfortable confines of the director's editing-projection room in New York City watching a scene from the latter part of *Life of Pi*. Joining them via video conference from Los Angeles were visual effects supervisor Bill Westenhofer and animation director Erik-Jan de Boer.

The scene conveyed how Pi's hard-won sense of mastery over the world is beginning to disintegrate under the pressure of day-to-day monotony and loneliness. Everyone watched Suraj Sharma crawl along the tarp of the lifeboat, imitating the motions and vocalizations of a tiger. Richard Parker lounges a few feet away.

"Richard Parker's rib cage should sync with Pi's," Lee said, and noted that not enough bones were showing at this point in the film. "Maybe Richard Parker shouldn't even be looking at Pi."

When Pi attempts to communicate, Lee asked, how should Richard Parker respond? How about a *prusten*—the quiet, puffing sound that tigers use to express friendliness or at least harmless intention. Squyres said, "I think the only thing Richard Parker is saying in this is, 'What are you saying?'"

"You talkin' to me?" someone joked, doing a street-tough tiger à la De Niro. There was a ripple of laughter.

In the end, the decision was no *prusten*. After all, Pi ends up getting on Richard Parker's nerves, and the tiger lunges at him.

Lee watched the rest of the scene. "The head movement is too big," he said. "We don't notice Richard Parker's eyes." This kind of detail is important because Lee wanted the audience to feel the impact of the big cat's presence on a subjective level. "And the tiger is too aggressive when he chases Pi," the director continued. "Richard Parker's scolding Pi—it shouldn't be too scary."

Over a two-hour period, the blocking of Richard Parker's movements—that is to say, the tiger's performance—was critiqued across the handful of scenes that were under review that day. Though the film was in post-production, it felt oddly as if Lee were giving notes to a live actor, one who was more responsive to instructions than a large, regal cat. Even though Le Portier has logged more time working with tigers than probably anyone alive, Lee had one big advantage over the trainer at this stage of the process, for he had almost fifty animators from the company Rhythm & Hues exclusively working

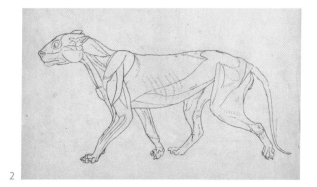

1

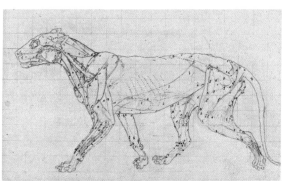

3

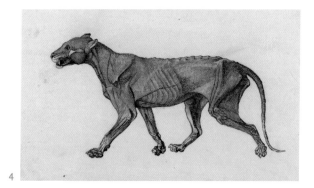

4

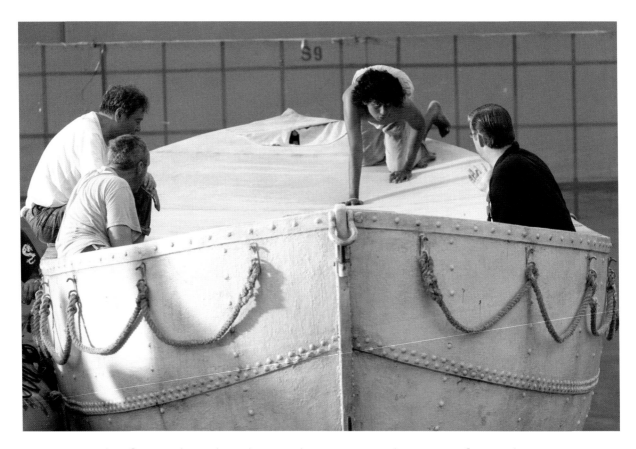

"I need to forget what I thought over the course—in this case—of more than a year. Or talked about, dreamed, and then prepped and shot. It takes about a month to forget about that, and just recognize what I have as the raw material."

—ANG LEE

on the actions of the tiger. Rhythm & Hues was creating a computer-generated (CG) cat that was photorealistically modeled on the real-life tiger King, but which could be made to do anything the filmmakers wanted him to.

So when Lee said that Richard Parker needed to tone down his aggression toward Pi in the talking scene, the animation company would provide him with a different take of the scene in which the tiger changed his movements accordingly, like a conscientious professional actor. If that take wasn't to Lee's liking, the tiger would play it differently for the next review, and the next one, until everything was as Lee wanted it to be.

Tim Squyres, Ang Lee's longtime editor, was of two minds about *Life of Pi*. From a traditional editing standpoint, Pi felt like less of a challenge for Squyres. Usually they shoot a whole bunch of coverage and they get it to me. And I figure

out how the scene's going to be constructed. Here, they're giving me a film where there's already a plan." The plan being the use of previsualization, which dictated most of the way the film was shot, except for the scenes in India and the framing narrative. Not that Squyres was completely constrained by that—he could certainly try to change things around—but because this was such a difficult, technical shoot, Lee and his crew were pretty economical with the footage.

PAGES 134–135: *Pi watches the Tsimtsum going down.* OPPOSITE: *Four plates from British animal painter George Stubbs's book* Structure of the Human Body with That of a Tiger and a Common Fowl (1795–1806). *Drawing on studies of tiger anatomy as well as empirical observations, the animators on* Life of Pi *were reverse anatomists, building the animal from the inside out as the image order shows.* ABOVE: *Pi of the tiger: Suraj Sharma practices his feline moves.*

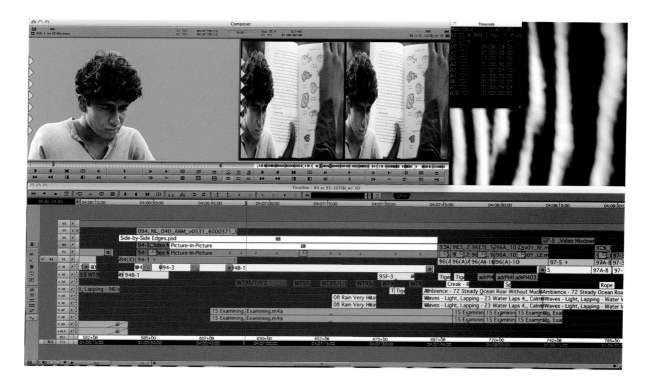

"In France we have a saying, *'Le metteur en scène c'est le bon Dieu'* [the director is the good Lord]."
—THIERRY LE PORTIER

There just wasn't that much extra material coming out of Taichung that an editor could play around with.

On the other hand, *Life of Pi* presented an amazing opportunity for an editor. In a normal film, Squyres says, "performances are what they are. I have seven takes and that's it. In *Life of Pi*, Richard Parker's not here yet. The waves aren't here yet. Production and post-production kind of blur together. On an effects film, like in *Hulk* or this, I get to be involved in creating a performance, which is a part of the job I'm not usually involved in."

Squyres talks about "tiger" and "waves" in the same breath as "performance." It might be strange to imagine Ang Lee, old-fashioned megaphone in hand to make himself heard over the roaring din, actually *directing* the waves—but that is in fact what he did, in a virtual sense, working with Moving Picture Company (MPC), the Vancouver-based effects house responsible for whipping up the two big storms (*Tsimtsum* and Storm of God). Lee dictated the basic shape of the waves before a mathematical simulation was run, so that the work of the special effects people had to answer both to the demands of the director's vision as well

as fit into the plausible parameters of how the ocean surface would behave under specific storm conditions. And that was no small order in what is probably the most complex type of special effect to begin with.

Though post-production was broken down into a series of subtasks spread out over several companies, for Lee and Squyres the post-production process started in postvisualization (postvis)—a sort of after-the-shoot version of previsualization—where modifications to existing images or the creation of new rough images of the tiger and other effects gave the editor and director something to work with. The two worked with the postvis artist to determine a rough blocking, a sense of where the tiger was going to be or move through the scene. This blocking served as a set of instructions for Rhythm & Hues, or as a basis of discussion.

ABOVE: *For the scene where Pi flips through the Survival Manual, editor Tim Squyres created a montage of Pi's expression while reading combined with images of the pages themselves.*

A SENSE OF PLACE

The India part of the film was all shot on location and was not effects-intensive except on a few occasions when, appropriately enough for this section of the story, more old-school techniques were used—matte painting (particularly for the backdrops in the Munnar sequence) and simple plates (that is, footage for the purpose of adding effects), which allowed a single shot or scene to be made of several separate components when practically or aesthetically required.

The biggest number of plates was required for one particular shot of the Pondicherry canal, the crossing that traditionally divided the French section from the Tamil (Indian) section in colonial days. This was supposed to be a brief glimpse of the city as it was in 1954, under French rule, but in reality, most of the old buildings are long gone from the intersection, trees have been planted that weren't there before, and so on. A set for the lower part of the old buildings was built in a parking lot outside of the city, and was shot as one plate; the upper stories, on another plate, were matte paintings by the effects company Crazy Horse; separate plates were also shot for different passers-by, as well as some plant details. This made for a total of six plates in all, which would be blended together—along with a computer-generated extension of the street and computer-generated water in the canal—into the final streetscape shown above: making this brief, unassuming glimpse of the colonial past the most complicated shot in the first, Indian act of the film.

The animators came back with roughed-out animations. "Sometimes they have better ideas than we do," says Squyres, "and we encourage them to." In the scene where Pi gives Richard Parker water to drink for the first time, Lee and Squyres had postvis of the tiger going straight for the bucket; but when they started blocking out the scene, the animators added a second or two of hesitation, the tiger tapping the unfamiliar receptacle a couple of times with his paws before slurping up the water. This heightened specificity gave the scene more character, and was more in line with a cat's instinctive caution when faced with an unfamiliar object.

The fact that animators often work on a single shot at a time may lead them to creative insights born out of minute attention to detail, but it can also make them think of the shot as an entity in itself. Says Squyres, "Like, 'this is the movie.' And sometimes [animators] won't want to end right in the middle of some action. But that's exactly what I want to do, because it leads right into the next shot." With each individual shot—that is, a length of footage from one cut to another—being worked on by a different individual animator or team of animators, there was plenty of room for variations to start creeping in—something for which Squyres, whose job it was to put all the cuts together into a coherent scene, had to be very much on the lookout.

Going over the animations is, in Squyres's words, "this endless back-and-forth for hundreds of iterations. Usually the animation comes first." But in fact, bits and pieces of the other elements start coming in as well. "In some instances we'll have some shots with waves that don't really have animation in them. And we'll have other versions of the same shots where you just see the walls of the wave tank behind, because it's different people working on it. Those all get merged together eventually."

Early rough cuts of effects-laden films are often an almost hallucinatory patchwork of all different stages. A real tiger, for example, might change into a crude previs tiger and then into a smooth, hairless tiger in the first stages of animation with someone in a blue-screen suit shimmering through the outline, all of these levels of image moving from one cut to another within a few seconds of a single scene—and with pool-ocean and blue-screen sky making similarly surreal transitions. As with all 3-D films, the process was refined again and again, layer by layer, until the stage called "finaling" was reached—the moment that Lee was able to look at a shot and say that a particular scene was done and ready to go into the movie. And that was for the visuals alone—scoring and sound design still had to come into play.

MAKING A SCENE

The process of putting together each shot was far from linear. In fact, all the elements of the film—and therefore the different departments in charge of handling them—were very much interdependent. In any given shot of *Life of Pi*, after all, the ocean reflects the sky, the sky determines the lighting, which in turn plays across the fur of the CG tiger, whose choreography is very much tied to the movement of the boat as it rides the waves, and so on.

Here is an example that illustrates some of the steps in the process of putting scenes together. These are bare-bones sketches, really, as the animation cannot be conveyed through stills.

This set of stills comes from the sequence in which Pi and Richard Parker are caught in a swarm of flying fish.

1. Plate: *The scene as it was shot with Sharma in the wave tank.* 2. Tracking: *The camera and boat movement is tracked to later match in the CGI elements.* 3. Animation: *Two different kinds: the hand-animated tiger (with basic skin texture) and individual, or "hero" flying fish (the background fish were procedurally animated using a software package called Massive).* 4. Tech animation: *The texture of the tiger's fur and details of his expression have been filled in, with skin and muscles added under the skin for greater realism.* 5. Lighting: *The silver and matte balls in the bottom left and the strip of fake tiger fur on the top left reference the reflections, shadows, and textures in the scene as shot on set, and were used for matching the lighting with the CG elements of the shot.* 6. Compositing: *All of the elements produced by other departments—tiger, fish, ocean, and sky—were blended and matched with the live footage.*

1

2

3

4

5

6

the vfx assembly line: who does what, or why end credits go on and on

As a computer-generated tiger, Richard Parker's central nervous system comprised a far-flung network of communication, computing, and creativity, stretching from New York to Los Angeles, by way of Mumbai and Hyderabad, Pi's homeland, where Rhythm & Hues also had animators working—whole teams of people working on every yawn, stretch, and leap, take after take, for weeks on end.

roaring water, flowing tiger: the animation pipeline

Rhythm & Hues created a specialized workflow to deal with the animation needs of *Life of Pi*, a film that operated under two particular conditions: 1) the fact that much of the film was shot on real water, which needed to be blended in varying degrees with CG water (except in the storm sequences, where it was entirely replaced); and 2) the fact that Richard Parker was both a real tiger and a computer-generated one, and that the cutting back and forth between the two had to be absolutely seamless.

The Shot Production Team

The shot production team made sure that the elements in the 3-D shots (right eye/left eye, color) were properly aligned and matched, and they made adjustments accordingly. Tracking took the live production footage and all the other data gathered on set (including camera movements, lenses, and so on) and matched those with the camera in the virtual world. Although the animators could move their characters in a "normal" virtual space from any perspective they chose, tracking ensured that the end result could then be re-matched with what was shot in the first place. The camera department did the virtual camerawork, working closely with the FX section of the water and sky team to create a feeling of ocean movement and drift—particularly

when the waves as shot in the tank had to be augmented, or when a scene was originally shot on a gimbal, whose mechanisms could never quite replicate the smooth ebb and flow of actual water. Final comp, or compositing, took every element produced for a shot by the other departments—ocean, sky, animated characters—and blended them with the live footage, ensuring that every component matched perfectly in order to produce the image that would end up on the movie theater screen.

The Water and Sky Team

The CG ocean section was in charge of water surface simulation, including parameters of height, basic lighting, and look. The art department handled the sky, taking images from HDRI (high dynamic range imagery) cameras that captured 360-degree views of the sky, and making any necessary adjustments and additions, such as cloud layers and movements. Special effects added spray, foam, and bubbles—all the details that give water its texture—and also oversaw the interaction of the CG water with the other elements such as the boat, the characters, and so on. Ocean lighting came in last, adding glints and highlights and bringing together all the ocean and sky special effects elements in the shot.

The Character Animation Team

Animation layout prepared the environment for the animator—that is, the spaces, surfaces, and objects with which the animator's characters (tiger, hyena, or other creatures) would interact. Animation was responsible for the actual choreography and physical movements of the tigers and other animal characters, working with relatively rudimentary, stripped-down versions. These would then be filled in by tech animation, who were responsible for simulating the muscle, skin, and fur that would give the characters the detail and texture of life. The respective roles of these two types of animators are analogous to those of the CG ocean and FX divisions of the water and sky team; and similarly, at the end of the line, character lighting lit all the characters in the animated shot to match the lighting that was used in the actual shoot.

reference, reference, reference

In the past, many of the other creatures that fell under Bill Westenhofer's supervision at Rhythm & Hues, like Aslan the lion in *The Chronicles of Narnia: The Lion, the Witch and the Wardrobe*, were required by their roles to smile or scowl, speak in the stentorian voice of Liam Neeson, and generally take on human or superhuman attributes. In *Life of Pi*, Richard Parker is required to do something that's in many ways more challenging in the context of Hollywood filmmaking: he must simply remain a tiger, true to his animal nature, just as King did on the set.

"The main challenge is to not overanimate," says animation supervisor Erik-Jan de Boer. "In terms of that feline-like motion, it is finding the proper balance. And again, we just use reference, reference, reference for all our stuff."

"It's to fight our own subconscious tendency to anthropomorphize things," says Bill Westenhofer. "By sticking doggedly to reference, we are keeping nuances and keeping subtleties of animalism in the performance." ("Bill is a real filmmaker," Lee says admiringly about Westenhofer's attention to detail.)

ABOVE: *The mighty reference.*

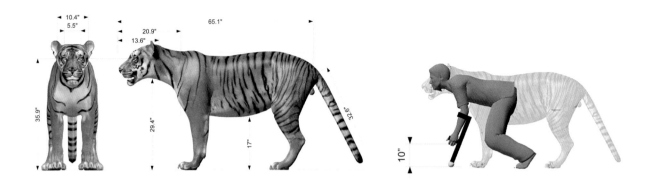

"The absolute ultimate goal of mine and the whole effects team
is to make it look like we did nothing at all."

—BILL WESTENHOFER, VISUAL EFFECTS SUPERVISOR

By "reference," de Boer and Westenhofer mean the hundreds of hours of video and thousands of photos that their team took of tigers, particularly of King. At the end of 2010, the two men began with a visit to Thierry Le Portier's compound, where they grabbed some initial still and video footage of King and Vlad, the hyena. De Boer returned to Los Angeles and started putting together a group of some forty-five animators—with teams in Los Angeles, Mumbai, and Hyderabad—to begin modeling the tiger.

Modeling means making sure the proportions and details of the real tiger are reflected in the digital model (skin and fur attributes come later, once the basic geometry has been established). "The tricky part is, of course, you're dealing with an animal that will not do what you're telling it to," says de Boer. "It won't sit still." (It will sometimes lunge at you, he forgets to add.)

De Boer went to Taiwan to capture more video reference and stills for the final, detailed modeling of the CG tiger. "Basically, I shot lots of close-ups of the nose for breathing patterns. Yawning and snarling and hissing and eating, drinking, grooming, marking. Sleeping, pissing. How does a paw change shape when it takes the weight? And how does it change shape when the weight rolls over it for a step? How do the nails protract and retract? Along with regular footage, De Boer stuck a single-lens reflex camera inside the boat and set it to snap away automatically while the tigers ran through their routines, enabling him to get some amazing close-ups without getting mauled.

All of these images and videos of King—as well as other tigers from a variety of outside sources—were then catalogued and broken down by category. There were pages of just snarls, tongue flicks, ear twitches, and so forth: any given shot might use references from several different sources. "And body wise, we tried to find the closest mechanical action we can, so we always have that reality check, that backup from reference, to find out if that is realistic, possible. Is this something that the animal can do?"

But the Richard Parker that appears on screen—the CG version—is not merely a Frankenstein patchwork of disparately sourced behaviors and gestures. About a third of the Richard Parker in *Life of Pi* is bona fide, flesh-and-fur tiger. And in many other shots, even when Richard Parker is fully computer generated, what you see is not based on what King might do, but what he (or Themis, or Minh, or Jonas) actually did. In those cases, the real tiger footage might have worked reasonably well, but needed some adjusting—either for a technical reason or for an aesthetic one—to heighten a subjective emotion, for example: "There are moments where Ang wants viewers to feel cinematically what they'd feel emotionally when they're facing a tiger," says Westenhofer, "so it was important to make sure the tiger's eye connected to the camera. A real tiger's never going to look at a camera in the same way it looks at the person it's facing off at." There isn't any very effective way to manipulate a shot of the real tiger so that it's looking in a different direction (for one thing, tigers turn their entire heads, not their eyes—to do the latter would seem, in Westenhofer's words, "really weird"). "So it'll be a CG tiger, and we're going to base our performance off of footage of a real tiger and make adjustments so the animal is looking at the lens." Since there's no way of switching in mid-stream, every shot is either strictly real or strictly digital, and the transition from one to the other is made in the cut.

In such cases, animators would often use virtual motion capture to translate a live tiger's performance into computer-generated imagery, matching every frame of a real shot with the CG tiger performing the same action, making whatever small changes that were necessary along the way (such as the adjustment of the gaze mentioned by Westenhofer), but otherwise staying as true as possible to all the movements and the physicality of the live animal footage.

fearful symmetry: king and richard parker

This is the story of two tigers.

One of them we know as King—the regal star of the tiger compound. King is flesh and blood.

The other tiger is called Richard Parker. Originally the star of a Man Booker Prize–winning novel, in which author Yann Martel sketched him in with a few brief descriptions (leaving the rest of him to take shape in the reader's imagination), Richard Parker underwent the long and arduous transformation from word to image, to be reborn as a computer-generated (CG) tiger. And he got his physical appearance—every last stripe of it—from King.

King was unaware of this. But there was a purpose to things they made King do, because pictures were being taken, measurements made, and teams of effects specialists halfway across the globe were already hard at work during the same time. A process had begun, at the end of which the real King would have an exact double in the virtual world; and without ever having met, the two tigers became as one in the film *Life of Pi*.

The first step in creating Richard Parker was modeling. To get King's basic proportions and details into the digital model of the tiger, the animators from Rhythm & Hues worked from the measurements and the reference photos and videos that de Boer and Westenhofer had taken of King at trainer Le Portier's compound.

Once his overall appearance was roughed out, two different teams of effects specialists worked on the realization of Richard Parker, who was built from the inside out. First in line were the animators, who constructed a skeleton, on which they added a layer of textured skin—with stripes, but no fur—to produce a plausible-looking tiger figure that they could move around for blocking out and choreographing each shot.

As Richard Parker's basic performance was being created by the animators (who were directed by Ang Lee), the second group, the technical animators, came in and added the subsequent layers to the computer-generated tiger: simulations of tiger muscle, skin, fur, and markings—all of which imparted texture, weight, and presence to Richard Parker.

Animation: Setting Richard Parker in Motion

Although a lot of research on tiger anatomy went into the building of the model, the virtual skeleton is not an anatomically correct tiger skeleton. It's a simplified structure, used to determine where the joint and pivot points would be for movement, and which parts would be visible through the layers of muscle and skin. "We used it as a structure to hang our other muscles and fat and skin jiggle controllers on," says de Boer.

Through the course of their teams' work, animation directors will often return to the skeleton as a point of reference. If there is any uncertainty about what an individual animator is doing, the shot can be done with just the skeleton as a way of double-checking that the motions are something that the animal would be capable of.

The next layer in building the digital tiger was textured skin animation. King's basic outline and markings were now in place as the computer-generated Richard Parker, but in a smooth, simplified form. "It looks like a tiger that's been shaved, basically," says Westenhofer. This was the figure that is used for blocking, the initial choreography that maps out where the animal is over the span of the shot—the rough action was then discussed and developed with the director.

Now came the work of refining the tiger's movements and placing him in the external world. In the case of Richard Parker, it meant creating his physical reactions to the environment around him, such as nausea in response to certain movements of the boat or a sense of instability when walking across the tarp. Behavioral gestures were put into place as well—for example, Richard Parker's tic, mentioned earlier, of tapping against the water bucket before taking a first drink. "We continue just finessing these details with the animators," Westenhofer says. "We talk to them about weight shifting, about where the weight is, about accelerations, about collisions and impacts, friction. There are facial details, too. Any overt physicality—that's what we're dealing with."

OPPOSITE: *An outtake from a project for using a person as a stand-in for the tiger—an idea that was scrapped in favor of stuffies.*

1

2

3

4

5

6

Technical Animation:
Giving Richard Parker His Stripes

While the skeleton-and-textured-skin version of Richard Parker was being run through his paces by the animation team and critiqued by Ang Lee, the groundwork was being prepared for the technical animators, who would start their work once the basic blocking of a shot or scene had been determined.

Technical animators specialize in the finer details of animation: muscle twitches and skin movement, the effect of wind on fur, gravity and motion on the flaps of loose skin that swing around the belly, the pressing of paws, and the protracting of claws. They also handle the interaction between the animal's volume and that of external objects—the impact of a collision with the sides of the lifeboat for example, or the press of the

animal's weight as it walks across the tarp. As the animators set the tiger in motion, the tech animators give it presence, and the muscles constitute the core layer in this process. The movement of the muscles is what determines the behavior of the CG animal's outer, visible layers—the surface of the skin (the twitches, contractions, and so on) and, on top of that, the fur.

Like the skeleton used by the animators, the CG tiger's muscles reflect not so much correct tiger anatomy as what's needed to achieve the moving, lifelike surface textures necessary for the CG King to match the real-life King as exactly as possible.

In the skin simulation, the layer that wraps over the muscles, the tiger's surface is marked not with stripes but with a fine grid, which helps the technical animators to evaluate what the skin is doing—where the surface is stretching, contracting, or wrinkling, depending on position and movement.

A slightly different epidermal view is provided by the simulated skin with grid tech—with the letter-filled squares, Richard Parker looks like some kind of walking newspaper puzzle, but the purpose of these labeled areas is actually to help tech animators to map out the tiger's color and stripe patterns.

Richard Parker finally got to put on a nice, warm layer in the fur simulation, but something was still not right: he was literally a white tiger, without so much as a single stripe. But this layer is purely about the texture of the tiger's coat, and how it moves under the influence both of inner (muscular contraction, twitching skin, and so on) and outer forces (wind, water, gravity, and so on).

Finally, with the lighting comes the colors and patterns, the glorious orange-and-black coat that makes the CG tiger look like a real tiger. Wearing King's clothes, Richard Parker was now ready for his close-up. And here is King once again: two tigers, one solid, one made of bytes. Which one is which?

Pi's Ark

The other animals on "Pi's ark," as Pi calls it, were all constructed using more or less the same technology as was used to build up the tiger.

With Hari the hyena, as with Richard Parker, the animators had a well-documented real-life referent to both work off and try to blend seamlessly with—Thierry Le Portier's hyena Vlad. A professional animator who appreciates a good kinesthetic challenge, de Boer says of hyenas: "In terms of their motion, they're very stiff-spined. They have strange proportion, with a heavy head on a long neck and those tiny little hind legs that are just very powerful. But they're sort of built to be always in a very balanced and secure frame on the ground.

OPPOSITE: *How to build a CG tiger, from the inside out: 1. Bones and skin animation. 2. Textured skin animation. 3. Muscle and bones simulation. 4. Simulated skin. 5. Simulated skin with grid tech. 6. Simulated fur.* TOP: *King (left) and RIchard Parker in his final stage.* ABOVE: *Mother and child orangutans from the Taipei Zoo, photographed as models for OJ.*

And that little seesawing acting that you get, with the head coming up and down, unweighting the hips so they can re-plant, you would almost want to compare it to how a giraffe moves. It's been a real fun challenge to try and get that into our animated hyena. It's very skittish, very nervous."

The other mammals in the film have more tenuous connections to specific real counterparts. OJ the orangutan is physically modeled on a female in the Taipei Zoo. The lame zebra in the boat has no specific real-life reference. Both the zebra and the orangutan are CG creations. The animators also worked on a few other larger CG mammals and CG birds—mixed in with real ones, shot in the Taipei Zoo—for the opening title montage.

Moving away from land required a different approach. "Fish are tricky," according to de Boer. "There's something about the buoyancy, and maybe it's the lack of motion—there is something that always makes it very easy to give away that these things were CGI or not realistic." Seeing the fish from above the water, refraction comes to the rescue with distortion and the proximity of above-water objects like the

raft for context. But getting the dorados, tuna, and other fish to look right underwater was more difficult. The dorado are mostly hand-animated, while the flying fish in the film are mostly controlled by a software package called Massive, which moves large quantities of figures within basic parameters, along with some hand-animated and even a few of the rubber ones that Sharma got pelted with by crew members during the shoot left in where appropriate.

storm of god, storm of ang

The Pacific Ocean is, of course, the other big star of *Life of Pi*, and in post-production the director's power expands from dominion over the animals to something truly godlike. The tank in Taichung, for all its impressive power, could only go so far in reproducing larger waves, and for the two key storm sequences—the sinking of the *Tsimtsum* and the Storm of God—the water shot in the tank was entirely replaced. It had to be: both events are hurricane-force storms—category twelve on the Beaufort scale, with thirty- to forty-foot waves. A Storm of God moment as shot in the tank versus what would eventually make it to the screen gives some idea of the difference in scale that was generated by the special effects work of Moving Picture Company (MPC). As for what it took to create such a virtual storm, the scale of the undertaking can be conveyed with a few brief statistics:

* A single shot of the *Tsimtsum* sinking sequence might contain as many as 269 million spray droplets.

* The ocean surface was resolved to details as small as two centimeters.

* A single second of complete ocean simulation could take up to seventy-two hours of computer-processing time.

* 786 texture maps—each one representing a particular surface (i.e., window pane, rusted steel panel, rope, etc.)—were used to render the *Tsimtsum* itself.

* And, most remarkable of all, *Life of Pi* was so big in terms of data that, MPC's 2011 jobs aside, *Life of Pi's* largest scene, the *Tsimtsum* sinking sequence, was the same size, if not larger, than all their previous jobs combined.

Why did these two sequences in *Life of Pi* require so much time and effort? As in pre-production, the answer is water. As in life, so in virtual reality: water, the most basic element to our existence, is fiendishly complicated and time-consuming to simulate and render. And the configuration of *Life of Pi* was made particularly difficult by the fact that so much of the movie takes place on the ocean and outside, with a nearly constant ocean backdrop and very low to the water: "The base of our shots is basically always moving," says MPC's visual effects supervisor Guillaume Rocheron.

The job also required a different methodology for MPC: usually, the company runs massive ocean simulations before designing the effects, using extremely powerful and specialized software from a company called Scanline to generate the waves in the most realistic way possible within a given set of parameters (that is, wind speed, ocean depth, weather, and so on). The animation and design of the shots normally follow.

But with *Life of Pi*, the entire *Tsimtsum* sinking sequence was already laid out in detail in previs; in other words, the Storm of God was basically the Storm of Ang, who carefully

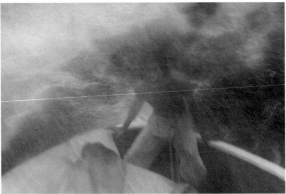

choreographed the chaos for maximum dramatic and aesthetic impact. But even while maintaining directorial control over the elements, Lee also wanted the highest possible degree of realism, from the biggest rogue wave to the tiniest fleck of foam: though orchestrated, the storm had to be as authentic as possible. And so MPC reversed the order in which they usually worked, doing the wave animations first, and running the simulations afterward, somehow endeavoring to insure that the ideal of the director's vision and the reality of the mathematical simulation meshed convincingly in the end.

A carefully composed, art-directed, but within specific parameters, highly realistic storm? "It's one of the hardest things to do in our industry, you know," says Rocheron. "But I think it's really one of the first films that we're actually pushing it that far. Because it's really having the photorealistic water, but being able to art-direct it completely so the waves, the events—everything—is driven by the story, not by the computer."

OPPOSITE: *Low-tech creative F/X: crew members pummel Suraj Sharma with rubber flying fish.* ABOVE: *Even cranked to maximum, the wave tank (top) had to be entirely replaced by CG waves (bottom) for the category twelve Storm of God.*

TS 270: anatomy of a shot

Perhaps the most choreographed shot in the entire film, the thirteen-second TS 270 (*Tsimtsum*, shot 270) happens as follows: a giant (fifty-foot) rogue wave lifts the lifeboat, with Pi clinging to the tarp, and slams against the top of the *Tsimtsum*—breaking the rudder and washing away some sailors on deck—then releases the lifeboat, which slides away from the sinking ship at enormous speed.

Because this shot consisted of a chain of specific incidents, it was designed before the production and supervised with the help of MPC.

In Taichung, the lifeboat sat on the giant gimbal with an additional rotating plate on top. The camera was mounted on a very large motion-control rig known as a bulldog crane. The shot is computer-generated imagery up to a point—that is,

everything, including Pi and the lifeboat—and then switches to live action when the camera gets very close. Rocheron explains: "We designed the shot in the computer, and then identified from where in that shot we could actually have Pi on the lifeboat, on the gimbal, and the camera programmed with the mover as a motion control running in sync so that it would make the lifeboat and the camera move exactly the same as in the computer-generated imagery." The shot was redesigned from the previs version to reflect the most realistic possible wave timings and sizes. The transition from digital lifeboat and digital Pi to live action takes place when the lifeboat hits the crane on top of the *Tsimtsum*. But, for the start of the shot, computer-generated imagery was necessary because there was no way to get a crane that was tall enough to shoot the boat going up and down a wave of that size.

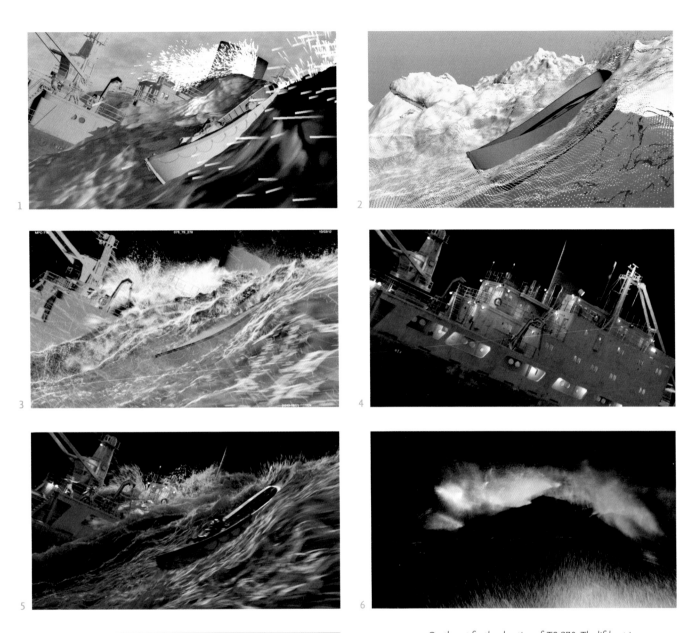

OPPOSITE: On the set for the shooting of TS 270. The lifeboat is on the largest gimbal, used for the Tsimtsum set. THIS PAGE: It's raining ones and zeros: whipping up a storm, layer by layer: 1. Shot layout. 2. Water surface simulation. 3. Spray simulation. 4. Tsimtsum render. 5. Water surface and boats render. 6. Interactive spray. 7. Final composite.

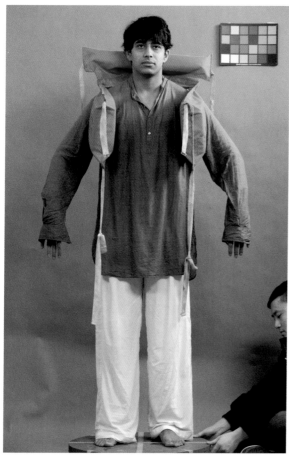

In order to get an exact match between the live shot and the CG version, a computer representation of the bulldog rig was used to design the camera moves and calculate the amount of track needed, among other things. This simulation was then exported into the real bulldog rig, which repeated the move exactly during the production.

So much for production: How was TS 270 put together in post-production? The work on any given shot that MPC did for *Life of Pi* could be broken down into a number of basic stages, a simplified version of which is presented here. The stills are shown from shot TS 270, but the stages and layers apply to most of the shots that MPC handled for the film.

As in the collaboration with Rhythm & Hues, the first layer was animation, in which the timings were blocked out and all the key elements (in this case, the boat, the rogue wave, the collision, and the sailors getting washed away) were coordinated to work together and within the context of the other shots in the sequence.

The shot's second layer was water simulation. Once the overall parameters were set for the shot, computers ran a massive fluid simulation to make the water surface behave like water, with properties of flowing, cresting, splashing, and so forth, within the particular context of deep open ocean in the grip of a category twelve storm.

The third layer was the simulation of ocean texture: spray, bubbles, and foam. This process was roughly analo-gous to the tech animation for Richard Parker, which added muscle, skin, and fur. When the ocean surface was ready (that is, the movements and shapes of the waves were established), then the computers simulated spray—which forms when the water reaches peaks or moves too fast. The spray goes back into the water surface, releasing bubbles, which in turn rise to the surface of the water as foam. These three elements form a cycle, which are part of the same simulation that "makes a realistic final ocean," says Rocheron.

Meanwhile, a CG lifeboat with a CG Pi, and a CG *Tsimtsum,* with richly detailed textures to match those of the original sets, were created for this part of the shot as well—elements that would be thrown into the seething, frothy mix.

In the next stage, the elements were assembled and lit together. What makes the *Tsimtsum* storm particularly fright-ening and chaotic is that it happens in the dead of night, so the only source of illumination is from the sinking ship itself. The final elements are then added, binding the whole storm shot together: rain and the wind are introduced into the scene, generating the last layer, mist, which obscures the vision and defines the turbulent, chaotic atmosphere.

artificial pi

In the months that he was on set, carrying the entire weight of the film, it seemed as if there was nothing Suraj Sharma couldn't do. But even he couldn't be everywhere at once, and for those few moments in the film where that was the case—shot TS 270 in the *Tsimtsum* sequence, a shot in Storm of God, and a couple of other instances where several shots had to be stitched together into a continuous action—a digital double was created. Unlike King, Sharma could easily be persuaded to go into a scanning machine and hold still for a few minutes, so the process of building the artificial Pi was fairly straightforward—the more so since the character would be used mostly in long shots, and did not require as fine a repertory of expressions as the CG Richard Parker.

To build Pi's digi-double, several techniques were used to record Sharma's features so that a puppet could be constructed and manipulated by the animator. Sharma traveled to Australia for a cyber-scan, a kind of laser imaging that captured his exact shape and a range of basic expressions. Sharma and the other actors involved in the *Tsimtsum* sequence who might need digital alter-egos had their photos taken while standing on turntables—literally nothing more than lazy Susans, slowly spun by hand to capture every side of the body. These were used as reference for skin and clothing textures. Bill Westenhofer arranged for what he calls "a poor man's motion capture"—a simple arrangement of three cameras to record some basic moves.

Another area in which computer-generated imagery came in handy was the enhancement of Pi's gauntness. For Pi's proclamation, "we're dying, Richard Parker" to resonate with any gravity, both he and Richard Parker had to look thinned down.

OPPOSITE TOP: *Suraj Sharma stands on a turntable, to be photographed from different angles for skin, hair, and clothing textures.*
OPPOSITE BOTTOM: *The resulting computer-generated animation.*
ABOVE: *Sharma with body double Ricky Peters.*

In the case of the tiger, Rhythm & Hues had the look all mapped out, with six different incarnations of the tiger's physique, beginning with an adolescent animal for the feeding cage scene, a tiger in the prime of life at the start of the journey, and then a tiger in four stages of decline, leading up to the skin and bones look of the landing in Mexico.

Suraj Sharma had to lose a fair amount of weight to play Pi. But there's a point in the story—after the Storm of God—beyond which special effects would have to take over from diet and exercise.

For the "we're dying" scene, the production turned to the effects house Lola, whose artists digitally massaged Suraj Sharma's photographic image until the desired look was achieved.

For the beach landing scene, the production found a suitable live double, a wiry South African named Ricky Peters, who happened to be working as a schoolteacher in Taichung. Peters was mainly in the shot where Pi has just pulled his boat onto shore and is lying collapsed on the sand. To substitute Suraj Sharma's face for Peters's face, a technique called face replacement was used. Lit and made up the exact same way as he would have been in the shot, Sharma re-enacted that moment in the film in a New York City studio, with Lee's direction and footage of Peters's performance as reference. The moving texture of Sharma's face was then tracked and projected onto a frozen digital head.

Something like face replacement would be truly uncanny, bordering on creepy, if it weren't so seamlessly done, and done for the greater purpose of the story—which at this point in the film lies in the relationship between what Pi is looking at—Richard Parker, poised at the edge of the jungle—and what the tiger does next.

And at that moment, Ang Lee does a very simple thing with the camera, creating a shift in the depth and color of the image to convey what happens, the feeling of what happens, and the higher narrative sense of it all. Never mind what it is, just watch for it—or better yet, don't watch for it, and in fact, ignore everything that you've read in this chapter.

In the end, after you've counted every droplet of water, split the tiger's most finely rendered whiskers, and marveled at what has been accomplished by teams of the best effects artists around—in the end you can forget all of it, because if they've done their job well, it will be invisible. *Life of Pi* will be just a boy in a boat: a story well told and believable up to a point, and beyond that point, moving enough that you will take the leap of faith and follow it all the way to its final moment. And then back to the beginning.

OPPOSITE: *Sharma reenacting his beach landing for facial capture.*
ABOVE: *Pi raises his head from the sand, looking for Richard Parker.*

COMING ASHORE: DIRECTING PI'S ARRIVAL IN MEXICO

Pi finally came ashore on a pristine stretch of southern Taiwanese sand (the Happy Panda campground in Kenting, which stood in for the Mexican coast). In real-world, shooting-schedule time, which didn't always follow the story's chronology, our hero would end up back in his lifeboat for a brief spell, and Sharma's most challenging acting moments still lay ahead. Nonetheless, there was a sense of arrival that day, a glimpse of honest-to-God sunlight at the end of the blue-screen tunnel, which made the crew nearly giddy with pleasure. Photographer Mary Ellen Mark came back for a few days and captured some of the mood and Ang Lee's fluid gestures as he enacted the sequence of Pi's arrival for the crew.

acknowledgments

In relation to its subject, this book is like a paper boat bobbing in the wake of a giant freighter. Still, it floats and follows the film; and for this, thanks are due to many people.

First to Fox, for facilitation, transportation, and a lot of illustration.

To the Davids who were onboard at the beginning: David Magee, genial traveling companion in India, collaborator in development, and purveyor of insight for the book; David Womark, who made many calls and told great tales; and above all, David Lee—as always, the hardest-working man in show business (except for those few months when Suraj Sharma was in the tank), and as always, the kindest—who made it really happen.

To Kho Shin Wong and Tiffanie Hsu, who helped me navigate around production and made the whole Taichung Airport experience seem a little less weird.

To everyone on set and off who gave valuable phone or face time, information, and visual material, including: Adil Hussain, Andrew Moffett, Arjun Bhasin, Avy Kaufman, Brian Cox, Brian Gardner, Charlie Croughwell, Claudio Miranda, David Gropman, David Ticotin, Drew Kunin, Eddie Maloney, Elias Alouf, Elizabeth Gabler, Fae Hammond, Gil Netter, Haan Lee, Joy Ellison, Katie Lee, Kevin Buxbaum, Kirsten Chalmers, Manning Tillman, Mary Cybulski, Michael Malone, Nitya Mehra, Rick Hicks, Robert Schiavi, Robin Miller, Robin Pritchard, Shailaja Sharma, Sled Reynolds, Steve Callahan, Suraj Sharma, Tabrez Noorani, Tabu, Thierry Le Portier, Victoria Rossellini, William Connor, and of course, Yann Martel.

For post-production, thanks to Bill Westenhofer (Rhythm & Hues), Erik-Jan de Boer (Rhythm & Hues), Guillaume Rocheron (MPC), Mychael Danna, Patrick Kearney (Rhythm & Hues), Tim Squyres, and, especially, Susan MacLeod, who patiently explained, showed me stuff, explained and explained again. Thanks also to everyone at the New York post-production office for leaving me a place at the lunch table.

As someone with a fairly rudimentary tech background, my main question while on set and in post-production was often, "What's this button for?" If I have ended up pushing any of the wrong ones in person or in print, the responsibility is entirely mine.

Many people gave me visuals for the book. Particular thanks to Wylie Griffin and the art department for all the great images that adorn the earlier parts of the book, especially to the still photographers Phil Bray, Peter Sorel, Jake Netter, and my dear friend Mary Ellen Mark, for making me agonize over which of the tens of thousands of fascinating photos I should select for the brief span of these pages; to Alexis Rockman for the scary, beautiful sketches and the chance to hang out in the lower depths; and to everyone in post-production for the stills which virtually bring the subject of special effects to life.

Grateful thanks to my editor at Harper Design, Elizabeth Viscott Sullivan, who edited my sometimes tardy text with a sharp eye and colorful balloon comments in the margins. I'd also like to thank Harper Design's art director Iris Shih and book designer Jason Snyder for putting everything in its place beautifully.

And as always, to the Writers' Room—for community, sanctuary, and a clean, well-lighted desk.

Deep gratitude and much else besides to my wife, Lisa, who gave me great editorial advice, and then reminded me which was the better story (the one with family); and to my boys August and Prosper, whose heads will be filled with dreams of shipwrecked boats, boys, tigers, and (this one's for you, Prosper) carnivorous islands in a couple of years' time—I can't wait.

And finally, with respect and affection to Ang Lee, who has always been an inspiration to work with, and who turned out to be a fascinating and generous subject to write about as well. This is his book.

photography and illustration credits

All film, VFX stills, storyboards, previsualizations, and set designs, as well as still photographs by Phil Bray, Peter Sorel, Jake Netter, and Mary Ellen Mark, © 2012 Twentieth Century Fox Film Corporation. All rights reserved.

2–3: Photograph: Jake Netter. **5:** Unknown artist. *The Hindu god Krishna and his consort sheltered from the rain by an umbrella.* c. 800–900. Himachal Pradesh, India. Opaque watercolor on paper. Gift of Mr. Johnson S. Bogart, F2003.34.25. © Asian Art Museum, San Francisco. Used by permission. **6–7:** Photographs: Peter Sorel. **8:** Unknown artist. Untitled (*Matsyavatara*). Late eighteenth century. India. Ink, gouache, and gold on paper, 7 ¾ x 5 ⁹⁄₁₆ inches. University of California, Berkeley Art Museum and Pacific Film Archive; gift of Jean and Francis Marshall. Photographed by Benjamin Blackwell. **11:** Unknown artist. *Vishnu and Lakshmi on the Great Snake.* Opaque watercolor on paper. Pahari style. c. 1870. Kangra, India. © Victoria and Albert Museum, London. **12–13:** Photograph: Phil Bray. **14–15:** Photographs: Mary Ellen Mark.

Chapter 1
16–17: Conceptual sketch: Alexis Rockman (watercolor and ink on paper). **18:** James Ricalton. *Famous "Man Eater" at Calcutta Zoo.* Photographic print. 1903. Copyright © The British Library Board, all rights reserved, photo 181/(50). **20:** Storyboards: Haan Lee. **21:** Comic book panels: Andrea Dopaso. **22:** Photographs: Phil Bray. **23:** Photograph: Mary Ellen Mark. **24–25:** Photograph: Peter Sorel. **26, top:** Unknown artist. Untitled (*Shiva's family*). 1730. India. Ink, gouache, and gold on paper, 11 ⁷⁄₈ x 8 ⁵⁄₁₆ inches. University of California, Berkeley Art Museum and Pacific Film Archive; gift of Jean and Francis Marshall. Photographed by Benjamin Blackwell. **26, bottom:** Composite elephant design: Joanna Bush. **27 and 28:** Photographs: David Magee. **29, top:** Photograph: Peter Sorel. **29, middle and bottom; 30, top:** Photographs: Jean-Christophe Castelli. **30–31, bottom:** Panorama: Jean-Christophe Castelli. **31, top:** Photograph: David Magee. **32, top:** Anonymous. *Landscape with Huge Banyan Tree Beside a River.* Watercolor. 1825. Copyright © The British Library Board, all rights reserved, Add.Or.2525. **32, bottom:** Unknown artist. *Vision of the Sage Markandeya.* India. c. 1775–1800. Opaque watercolor and gold on paper, 11 ½ x 9 ¼ inches. Mat: 11 ⅜ x 9 ³⁄₁₆ inches. Philadelphia Museum of Art: purchased with the John T. Morris Fund, 1955. **32–33:** Photograph: Mary Ellen Mark. **34–35:** 3-D sketches: Brian Gardner. **36:** Photograph: Peter Sorel. **37:** Photograph: Phil Bray. **38, top:** Photograph: Jean-Christophe Castelli. **38, middle:** Photograph: Peter Sorel. **39:** Stills from previsualizion by Halon Entertainment. **40:** Illustrations: Haan Lee. **41:** Island conceptual sketches: Alexis Rockman (watercolor and ink on paper). **42, top:** Painting: *Manifest Destiny*, by Alexis Rockman (oil and acrylic on panel), 2003–4. **42, bottom and 43:** Island conceptual sketches: Alexis Rockman (watercolor and ink on paper).

Chapter 2
44–45: Photograph: Peter Sorel. **46:** Unknown artist. *Composite Man and Tiger.* c. 1750–1800. Northern India. Opaque watercolor on paper. Gift of Mr. and Mrs. George Hopper Fitch, 1988.51.12. © Asian Art Museum of San Francisco. Used by permission. **47:** Photograph: Tiffanie Hsu. **48:** Chinese calligraphy: Ang Lee. **49:** Photograph: Thierry Le Portier. **50–51:** Photograph: Peter Sorel. **52:** Photograph: David Gropman. **53:** Photographs: Peter Sorel. **54:** Time-lapse photographs: Josh Smith. **55, top:** Wave chart: Steven Callahan. **55, bottom:** Photograph: Robin Miller. **56, left:** Photograph: Peter Sorel. **56, right:** Boat movement chart: Tiffanie Hsu. **57, top and middle:** Photographs: Peter Sorel. **57, bottom:** Photograph: Jake Netter. **58:** Photographs: Peter Sorel. **59:** Photograph: Jake Netter. **60:** Thomas Daniell. *Hindoo Temple at Agouree, on the River Soane, Bahar.* Colored aquatint. 1796. Copyright © The British Library Board, all rights reserved, P929. **61, top:** Photographs: Peter Sorel. **61, bottom:** Photograph: Susan MacLeod. **62–63:** Photographs: David Gropman. **64:** Photograph: Tiffanie Hsu. **65, top:** Photograph: Peter

Sorel. **65, bottom:** Drawing: Sarah Contant. **66:** Photographs: David Gropman. **67, top:** Drawing: Jim Hewitt. **67, bottom:** *Tsimtsum* poster: illustration by Chen Hui; layout by Joanna Bush. **68 and 69, bottom:** Lifeboat charts: *Life of Pi* art department. **69, top:** Lifeboat models: Scot Erb. **70, top and bottom left:** Photograph: Haan Lee. **70, middle and bottom right:** Photographs: Peter Sorel. **71, top:** Life raft chart: *Life of Pi* art department. **71, bottom:** Photographs: Peter Sorel. **72:** Photomontage of chart by Steven Callahan: Jean-Christophe Castelli. **73:** Photograph: Jake Netter. **74–75:** Drawings: Steven Callahan. **76–77:** Survival manual illustrations: Joanna Bush. **78:** Photograph: Jean-Christophe Castelli. **79, top:** Photograph: Jake Netter. **79, bottom:** Photograph: Jean-Christophe Castelli. **80–81:** Photograph: Tiffanie Hsu.

Chapter 3
82–83: Photograph: Peter Sorel. **84:** Eadweard Muybridge. *Animal Locomotion*, plate 729 (Tigress Walking). University of Pennsylvania Archives. **85:** Photographs: Phil Bray. **86–87:** Photographs: Jake Netter. **88, top:** Photograph: Phil Bray. **88, bottom:** Photograph: Jake Netter. **90, top:** Photographs: Phil Bray. **90, bottom:** Photograph: Jake Netter. **91:** Photograph: Phil Bray. **92, top:** Photograph: Jake Netter. **92, bottom and 93, top:** Photographs: Phil Bray. **93, bottom:** Photograph: Mary Ellen Mark. **94, top:** Photographs: Phil Bray. **94, bottom and 95, top:** Photographs: Peter Sorel. **95, bottom:** Photograph: Tabrez Noorani. **96:** Photographs: Mary Ellen Mark. **97:** Photographs: David Gropman. **98, top:** Photograph: Jake Netter. **98, bottom and 99, top:** Photographs: Mary Ellen Mark. **99, bottom and 100–1, top:** Photographs: Peter Sorel. **100–1, bottom and 102:** Photographs: Phil Bray. **103:** Photograph: David Gropman. **104, top and middle:** Photographs: Peter Sorel. **104–5 and 106, top:** Photographs: Jake Netter. **106, bottom:** Photograph: Mary Ellen Mark. **107, top** Photograph: Peter Sorel. **107, bottom:** Photograph: Mary Ellen Mark. **108–10 and 111, top:** Photographs: Peter Sorel. **111, bottom:** Still courtesy of Twentieth Century Fox. **112–13 top:** Illustration: Joanna Bush. **112, bottom:** Photograph: Jake Netter. **113, bottom:** Flyers: Katie Lee. **114, top:** Photograph: David Lee. **114, bottom:** Photograph: Jake Netter. **115, top:** Photograph: Peter Sorel. **115, bottom and 116:** Photograph: Jake Netter. **117, top:** Photograph: Peter Sorel. **117, bottom:** Photograph: Jake Netter. **118:** Photograph: Peter Sorel. **119, top and middle:** Photographs: Peter Sorel. **119 bottom and 120, top:** Photographs: Jake Netter. **120, middle and bottom:** Stills courtesy of Twentieth Century Fox. **121–25:** Photographs: Peter Sorel. **126, top:** Photograph: Mary Ellen Mark. **126, bottom:** Photograph: Jake Netter. **127, top:** Photograph: Mary Ellen Mark. **127, bottom–128, top:** Photographs: Peter Sorel. **128, bottom:** Still courtesy of Twentieth Century Fox. **129, top:** Photograph: Jake Netter. **129, bottom–133:** Photographs: Mary Ellen Mark.

Chapter 4
134–135: Still courtesy of Twentieth Century Fox. **136:** George Stubbs. Four drawings from *A Comparative Anatomical Exposition of the Structure of the Human Body with that of a Tiger and a Common Fowl.* Graphite on paper. Yale Center for British Art, Paul Mellon Collection. **137:** Photograph: Peter Sorel. **138:** Editing screen by Tim Squyres. **139:** VFX stills: Rhythm & Hues. **141:** VFX stills: Rhythm & Hues. **143:** Photograph: Erik-Jan de Boer. **144:** Illustrations: Rhythm & Hues. **146–47, top:** Tiger build VFX stills: Rhythm & Hues. **147, bottom:** Photograph: Susan MacLeod. **148:** Photograph: Peter Sorel. **149:** VFX stills: The Moving Picture Company. **150:** Photograph: Jake Netter. **151:** VFX stills: The Moving Picture Company. **152, top left and bottom left:** Pi digital double: The Moving Picture Company. **152 bottom, right:** Cyberscans: Headus. **153:** Photograph: Mary Ellen Mark. **154, top:** Photograph: Kho Shin Wong. **154, middle and bottom:** VFX stills: Lola. **155:** Photograph: Peter Sorel. **156–57:** Photographs: Mary Ellen Mark.

160: Photograph: Mary Ellen Mark.

HarperCollins books may be purchased for educational, business, or sales promotional use. For information please write: Special Markets Department, HarperCollinsPublishers, 10 East 53rd Street, New York, NY 10022.

First published in 2012 by
Harper Design
An Imprint of HarperCollinsPublishers
10 East 53rd Street
New York, NY 10022
Tel: (212) 207-7000
Fax: (212) 207-7654
harperdesign@harpercollins.com

Distributed throughout the world by
HarperCollinsPublishers
10 East 53rd Street
New York, NY 10022
Fax: (212) 207-7654

ISBN 978-0-06-211413-6
Library of Congress Control Number: 2011931359

Book design by Jason Snyder

Printed in the United States of America

First Printing, 2012